Warlpiri karnta karnta-kurlangu yimi

Warlpiri
WOMEN'S VOICES

Other books in the Oral History Series:

Long Time, Olden Time: Aboriginal accounts of Northern Territory history, collected and edited by Peter and Jay Read

Kaytetye Country: An Aboriginal history of the Barrow Creek area, compiled and edited by Grace Koch.

Warlpiri karnta karnta-kurlangu yimi

Warlpiri WOMEN'S VOICES

Our Lives Our History

Stories told by Molly Nungarrayi, Rosie Nungarrayi, Milly Nangala,
Topsy Nangala, Lady Nampijinpa, Lucy Nampijinpa and Kitty Napangardi
Transcribed and translated by Valerie Peterson Napanangka, Georgina
Napangardi, Janet Nakamarra Long, Violet Nampijinpa Downs
and Maisie Napaljarri Kitson
Collected by Georgina Napangardi, Janet Nakamarra Long and
Petronella Vaarzon-Morel
Compiled and edited by Petronella Vaarzon-Morel

IAD PRESS
ALICE SPRINGS

First published in 1995 by
IAD Press
PO Box 2531
Alice Springs
NT 0871
Phone: (089) 511 311
Fax: (089) 522 527

National Library of Australia cataloguing-in-publication data:

Warlpiri Women's Voices

ISBN 0 949659 75 4

1. Warlpiri (Australian people). 2. Warlpiri (Australian people) – Social conditions. 3. Warlpiri (Australian people) – Social life and customs. 4. Warlpiri (Australian people) – Rites and ceremonies. 5. Aborigines, Australian – Women – Northern Territory. 6. Aborigines, Australian – Women – Northern Territory – Biography. I. Vaarzon-Morel, Petronella. II. Nungarrayi, Molly. III. Title: Warlpiri women's voices.

306.0899915

Translators and transcribers of Warlpiri include Valerie Peterson Napanangka, Lee Cataldi, Georgina Napangardi, Janet Nakamarra Long, Violet Nampijinpa Downs and Maisie Napaljarri Kitson

Designed by Christine Bruderlin and Brenda Thornley
Map by Brenda Thornley
Cover linocut by Carole Napaljarri Kitson, cover photographs by Petronella Vaarzon-Morel
Photographs by Petronella Vaarzon-Morel except for the photographs on pages 107 and 108
Linocuts by Violet Nampijinpa Downs, Maisie Napaljarri Kitson and Carole Napaljarri Kitson
Printed by Australian Print Group

Contents

Part Three
Changes

Nyiyakurlu

Jinta
**Purami karlipa-jana ngalipa-nyangu purlka-purlka. Kuja
kalalu nyina ngurungka yupujurla.**

Jirrima
Nyurruwarnupatu: kamparruwarnu kardiyapatu

Wirrkardu
Kurruly-yirrarni

Acknowledgements

This book is for the women of Willowra, whose friendship and hospitality over the years have been as unceasing as their generosity in teaching me about Warlpiri culture. I particularly want to thank Molly Nungarrayi, Rosie Nungarrayi, Milly Nangala, Lady Nampijinpa, Lucy Nampijinpa and Kitty Napangardi, whose voices are heard in these pages. They graciously spent many hours helping Georgina Napangardi, Janet Nakamarra Long and myself record the stories. To their families I also want to extend my thanks. This book is a result of the efforts of many people, and without their interest and many kindnesses it could not have been written. Peggy Nampijinpa and Dora Napalajarri, in particular, were wonderful in their support.

I thank especially Georgina Napangardi and Janet Nakamarra Long for their tireless efforts in helping this project become a reality. In addition to helping tape, transcribe and translate the women's stories, we spent many hours together hunting, collecting firewood and sharing life experiences. Their friendship has enriched me greatly.

I am grateful to Willowra School for providing me with practical assistance during the project. Special thanks are due to Sean Ryan and to Jenny Mandersloot. Thanks are also due to Valerie Peterson Napanangka of Lajamanu and Lee Cataldi. Valerie helped transcribe and translate the Warlpiri stories; Lee also helped with the work. I also want to thank Connie Nungarrayi for assisting with the Warlpiri trancriptions, and David Nash for his comments on the transcriptions and translations.

I gratefully acknowledge the financial assistance of the Australian Institute of Aboriginal and Torres Strait Islander Studies and the Institute for Aboriginal Development. Without the continuing enthusiasm and forbearance of the staff of the Institute for Aboriginal Development, this work would not have been completed. In particular, thanks are due to Russell Goldflam and Mark MacLean. Russell helped initiate the project and sought funding to develop the initial manuscript for publication. Mark saw the project to fruition. My thanks also to Janet Blagg, editor-in-residence, and Brenda Thornley, illustrator and designer, at the Institute for Aboriginal Development, for their assistance in the final stages.

I would like to extend my thanks to Grace and Harold Koch, who generously shared their ideas with me and provided valuable comments on the initial manuscript. Thanks also to Tim Rowse for his comments on the latter. Special thanks go to Jim Wafer for his part in the project. He provided valuable editorial assistance and maintained a continuous belief in the value of the work. Finally, my thanks to David Avery for his support during the later stages of the project, and to little Marcelis for his good humour.

Petronella Vaarzon-Morel

Introduction

Warlpiri Women's Voices is a collection of narratives concerning the lives of a number of senior Warlpiri women from Wirliyajarrayi (Willowra), on the Lander River, in the Northern Territory of Australia. The speakers are Molly Nungarrayi, Rosie (Ruth) Nungarrayi, Topsy Nangala, Milly Nangala, Lady Nampijinpa, Nampijinpa, Nungarrayi, Kitty Napangardi and Lucy Nampijinpa. Their stories recount aspects of daily life before European occupation of their country, as well as their reflections on changes since that time. The women range in age from the mid-fifties to mid-eighties. Their memories of growing up, of learning about social relationships, religious ceremonies and how to hunt and gather are shaped by lives lived on the land. Through their stories we come to learn about Warlpiri social practices and how they are informed by complex cultural understandings of the meaning of the land. It is against this background that we read about the early encounters with Europeans, and the changing social and economic relations that followed.

In describing the first sustained contact with Europeans, the women tell of indignities endured at the hands of white men intent on establishing cattle runs on their land. We are given insights into the strategies Warlpiri used to continue living on their country while under threat of violence from whites. Through the women's narratives we come to understand something of how they responded to pastoralists and government practices in the post-contact period. Such practices included the provision of rations, the use of Aboriginal labour for stock and domestic work, the establishment of a school, and the introduction of new foods and medicines. The women also speak of their hopes for their children and future generations.

The voice of Petronella Vaarzon-Morel, who has known the women for two decades and is now an anthropologist, is also heard. I have compiled and edited the book and written the commentaries which accompany the translated and transcribed texts.

The writing of the book

This book is the result of a collaboration with the women over a long period of time. The idea initially arose in late 1987, when the Institute for Aboriginal Development (IAD) invited me to submit a proposal for a study of the impact of social and economic changes on Aboriginal women, to be funded by the United Nations Educational, Scientific and Cultural Organisation (UNESCO). At the time I was pursuing anthropological research with people at Willowra. I discussed the project with a group of senior women from the community whom I knew well, and we decided to submit a proposal to document women's knowledge about the past and their perceptions of change. We would record the women's stories on tape, then prepare written translations with accompanying commentaries. At the time, the women wanted their history recorded for their children and those who followed. They also hoped that, by speaking out, they might provide Europeans with some understanding of their relationship to the land and their culture, a relationship that has survived the changes wrought by the European political economy.

Although funding was limited, it would be sufficient to enable the recording of a selection of oral narratives which could be translated into written English texts with an accompanying commentary. The Warlpiri narratives and written texts would be made available for use in the school at Willowra. The project was considered to be of value to the community and was approved at a Community Council meeting, with Bandy Jakamarra Long presiding as president. We were funded for six weeks' work, and the telling of the stories began. The women chose co-researchers Georgina Napangardi Martin and Janet Nakamarra Long to help me record and translate the oral histories. Closely related to the storytellers, Georgina and Janet were employed at the time as literacy workers in the school's bilingual program.

The stories were recorded at Wirliyajarrayi (Willowra), an Aboriginal community located approximately 350 kilometres north-west of Alice Springs, in Central Australia. The name Wirliyajarrayi comes from a waterhole and important dreaming site on the Lander River, and has come to refer to both the Aboriginal village or 'community' located nearby, and to the area once encompassed by Willowra Pastoral Lease, now held by the Wirliyajarrayi Aboriginal Land Trust. The Lander River (Yarlalinji in Warlpiri) flows through Wirliyajarrayi from Mount Barkly in the south to the floodout in the Tanami Desert in the north. It is this general area that provides

Molly Nungarrayi, consumate storyteller and person of great knowledge and dignity, records narratives about her youth.

the setting for the stories. The region is the traditional home of Yalpari or Lander Warlpiri and, with the exception of Kitty Napangardi, who is Yanmajirri, the storytellers all speak Warlpiri as their first language. The Warlpiri women who tell the stories are senior members of Willowra community and are considered locally to be highly knowledgeable about women's Law and cultural issues.

In Warlpiri society knowledge of religious stories, songs and ceremonies that are associated with particular areas and sites on the land is passed orally from generation to generation. This knowledge is about the meaning of country. It differentiates groups of people from each other and defines their rights to land and its resources. Such knowledge is never the sole possession of an individual but is held by a network of people. Only those people who have the right to speak about Warlpiri Law and country may do so.

The imparting of knowledge about the more recent history of the Lander Warlpiri region is also subject to cultural constraints, although in this case they are less clearly defined. These constraints exist because stories about the past are also stories about people and country. A person's life trajectory is intertwined with geographical space and the events that have taken place in this space. These events may have occurred in the creative period of the Warlpiri world known as Jukurrpa (Dreaming), or in the course of everyday life. Over time, memory of the two may merge. Historical narratives are thus also discourses on identity, country and social relations. They are not just 'yarns' about the past, to be recounted by anyone. The storytellers must have 'been there', or, at least, been told the story by someone who was there.

The Warlpiri storytellers in this book have a profound and lifelong connection to Lander Warlpiri country. As traditional owners, they have authority to talk for the land and the historical events that have taken place on it. Together with their male relatives, they have the right to create public representations of the meaning of their country. Although the story-tellers' views tend to be representative of women of their age group with similar historical experiences, they do not always have a unified voice. People are affected in different ways by the same historical events and have differing interpretations of what happened.

The narratives should be read as a partial history of the Lander Warlpiri. They are not the totality of the stories the women can tell. Nor are the women the only ones who can tell stories about the past. A number of senior Warlpiri men have recounted narratives that appear in other oral history publications.[1]

We recorded the majority of the narratives 'out bush', away from the hustle and bustle of everyday life at Willowra. The mode of storytelling was similar to that used by women in the recounting of traditional narratives, in that the stories were told within a group that reflected the women's interrelationships with country.[2] The women defined the choice of topics. They also ordered the telling of the stories according to a rough chronology of life before contact; during the early days of white occupation, and in the quieter times during and after the Second World War. There were minimal interruptions and questions from the listeners as the women recounted their experiences. For the most part, the narratives were delivered in Warlpiri. The exception occurred in the case of Kitty Napangardi's stories. Kitty's first language is Yanmajirri, a language that neither Janet, Georgina nor I speak, so Kitty chose to tell her stories in Aboriginal English. Kitty's narratives also took the form of a dialogue with Georgina and myself rather than a monologue. The Warlpiri stories were told magisterially, in the style of traditional verbal arts. Unfortunately, the texts reproduced in this book cannot convey the intonations, facial expressions, body language and Warlpiri sign language used so creatively by the women during their performances.

After working intensely for the allocated time, Georgina, Janet and I produced a report and made copies available to members of the community, Willowra School and IAD. Immense interest in the women's narratives was shown at Willowra, and they were read and re-read until copies of the report fell apart. Because the storytellers are illiterate, the accounts were read aloud to them in English by younger, literate relations. At times they were re-translated orally into Warlpiri for the benefit of listeners who had little English. The readings usually took place in small gatherings, at some of which I was fortunate to be present. They were performative events in themselves. On hearing their stories read out, the storytellers typical-ly commented that they were 'true' and that, indeed, the events had happened as they had told. People nodded sadly at accounts of death and killings; all thought hilarious the story about the first sighting of an aeroplane, and the reader was asked to tell it again and again. The reading of the stories prompted the recounting of related incidents and the fleshing out of details merely hinted at in the original. Many of the storytellers used Warlpiri sign lan-guage to sign parts of their stories as they were read out, underlining the truth of their

---

[1] See, for example, Read and Read, 1991.

[2] Warlpiri relationships to land involve religious and social responsibilities which are shared between people who are linked by descent. The responsibilities of a person whose descent is traced through the father (*kirda*) are dif-ferent and complementary to those of a person whose descent is traced through the mother (*kurdungurlu*). Both *kirda* and *kurdungurlu* for the Wirliyajarrayi area were present for the telling of these stories.

accounts. Milly Nangala re-enacted several of her narratives, using body language of the style characteristic of women's dance performances. Thus the past was actively remembered. Despite the poverty of writing as a mode of representing Warlpiri arts of narration, people were not limited by the texts, but entered into dialogue with them.

The response of a number of Aboriginal people involved in tertiary studies in Alice Springs was encouraging, as was the interest shown by non-Aboriginal people working in Warlpiri communities in Central Australia. At that time there was very little published local Aboriginal history, and even less that specifically presented the views of Aboriginal women. Yet there was a demand for such material. As a result, the report was used extensively in Aboriginal Studies courses at IAD. The report came to the attention of government departments, and, for a while, senior women living at Willowra were increasingly consulted about their needs. Attempts were made to improve the living conditions of older women within the community by ensuring that they had access to water, firewood and transport. Their request for a women's centre was finally heeded, and funds made available for its operation. The women felt that their voices were being heard. Unfortunately, factors such as the frequent changes of non-Aboriginal staff at Willowra and the shifting political agendas of government agencies mean that women's voices are in constant danger of going unheard again.

Georgina, Janet and I felt that the publication of the stories as a book would ensure the voices of the women would not be lost. For their part, the storytellers considered their knowledge to be relevant to the present. Although the women had grown up in an oral tradition, many of their children and grandchildren have learned to read and write at school, and they now live in a partially literate Warlpiri society. They have long recognised the need for literature that would reflect their views, as a counter to those of the dominant society. They are also mindful of the power of the written word and of its capacity to be used by outsiders (both Aboriginal and European) to weaken local authority structures. By mapping the past they would be providing ways to think about the present.

As a result of local interest in the report and numerous outside requests for copies, we sought funding to publish the women's narratives in a different format. A small grant from the Australian Institute for Aboriginal and Torres Strait Islander Studies (AIATSIS) enabled work to begin. Staff at the Willowra and Lajamanu schools' vernacular literacy centres agreed to help with the lengthy process of transcribing the texts; Valerie Peterson Napanangka made a sterling contribution at Lajamanu, with the assistance of Lee Cataldi, transcribing the texts and providing written English translations. Unfortunately, other pressing curriculum concerns at Willowra meant that there were not as many transcriptions completed as we had hoped. As a result, we have more English-only texts than intended. In the meantime, Janet, Georgina and I taped, transcribed and translated some additional oral narratives. We rechecked our original written translations of the Warlpiri with the narrators; the style of language and choice of words used in the translations are a result of this collaborative process. The translations also reflect the fact that Georgina and Janet speak standard English. Although they understand it, they do not speak Aboriginal English.

Because of the interest shown by literate Warlpiri, and others, in the historical data contained in the commentaries to the original work, I decided to develop these further. At the same time, I did not want to drown out the storytellers' voices, nor turn the manuscript into an ethnographic treatise. For those who wanted more cultural background to the texts, there was already an abundance of ethnographic material on Warlpiri culture. In keeping with the style of the other oral histories published by IAD (*Long Time, Olden Time* and *Kaytetye Country*), the commentaries are limited to providing some brief contextual information.

Sadly, while the narratives were being prepared for publication, two of the storytellers died. In keeping with Warlpiri custom, we left discussing what should be done with their texts until some time had passed. We were later given permission to use some of their texts, provided we made no mention of their personal names and left out certain details. As a result, only the authors' skin names[3] appear on the texts in question.

As time went by the manuscript took on a substantially different form to the original report and became, in fact, a new work. A draft of the manuscript was read and commented on by Janet Nakamarra, who wanted to use it in an Aboriginal Studies course she was conducting for Kooris. Shortly afterwards, I was invited by Batchelor College to teach the Aboriginal Languages Fortnight at Willowra, and worked with a talented group of Warlpiri teacher and teacher-linguist trainees, including Violet Nampijinpa, Carol Napaljarri, Aileen Napaljarri, Judy Napaljarri, Audrey Napaljarri and Selma Nampijinpa. As the requirements for the course included students' reading examples of written Warlpiri texts and working on transcriptions and translations, I introduced the students to the draft narratives of this book. We had great pleasure in reading the texts and an exciting dialogue developed. They learned new things about their mothers' lives and the challenges they faced. They rediscovered words such as *kantirirri*, the traditional mortuary platform that was placed in a tree and on which the dead body was laid; and in learning these words, they began to explore other aspects of the past. In concert with the storytellers, we verified the Warlpiri transcriptions and the translations. A number of the Warlpiri texts contained some English expressions and Warlpiri renditions of English. The Warlpiri speakers wanted to replace these expressions with 'proper' Lander Warlpiri so that the texts would contain 'strong' Warlpiri: they wanted the texts to be more 'true' than the originals. The storytellers requested some other minor changes to their stories, which included the omission of some parts of the original narratives that might, they felt, cause offence. There was considerable discussion about the English translations of the Warlpiri, and changes were also made in this area. That the English translations are free rather than literal and interlinear reflects the fact that they were largely translated by Warlpiri who are not linguists.

Where parallel translations are provided, these have been set out so that corresponding paragraphs are aligned for ease of comparing the texts. In a number of cases the English translations are condensed versions of the Warlpiri, some of the repetition having been left out.

Kitty Napangardi's stories are told in Aboriginal English, a form of English related to the Pidgin English used by Aborigines and Euro-Australians to communicate with one another in the first decades after contact. Grace Koch provides an overview of the features of Aboriginal English in *Kaytetye Country*, the second book in the IAD oral history series, and the reader is referred to this work for a guide to reading this dialect.[4]

Warlpiri words are italicised at their first use (and throughout the book if they occur only sporadically); they and some Aboriginal English terms are defined in the glossary.

---

[3] Classificatory names; see 'Aboriginal skin names', page xiv

[4] Koch, 1993: x.

Aboriginal skin names

The reader will notice that the storytellers and other Warlpiri mentioned in this book have both English and Warlpiri names. The Warlpiri names are not surnames in the European sense, but names that classify each individual in Warlpiri society in relationship to other people, to the Jukurrpa, and to the land.

These names are called 'skin names' in Central Australia, and 'subsection names' in the anthropological literature. The skin system is a shorthand version of the complex Warlpiri kinship system, and facilitates the working out of rights and obligations in relation to other people — for example, which individuals one may marry.

Men's names begin with *J* and women's with *N*. The names are as follows:

Male	*Female*
Jangala	Nangala
Jampijinpa	Nampijinpa
Jupurrula	Napurrula
Jakamarra	Nakamarra
Jungarrayi	Nungarrayi
Japaljarri	Napaljarri
Japanangka	Napanangka
Japangardi	Napangardi

The male skin names above are grouped into father-son pairs, so that, for example, Jangala's son is Jampijinpa, and Jampijinpa's son is Jangala. The eight skin names that come first in each pair form one 'generation level', while the eight skin names that come second in each pair form the other generation level. A person should marry someone from their own generation level. The four pairs of skin names at the top of the list form one half of Warlpiri society, called a 'moiety' in the anthropological literature, and the four pairs at the bottom form the other half. A person should, ideally, marry outside their own moiety.[5]

The symbol = links first choice marriage partners in the following diagram:

J/Nampijinpa	=	J/Napangardi
J/Nakamarra	=	J/Napaljarri
J/Napurrula	=	J/Napanangka
J/Nangala	=	J/Nungarrayi

---

[5] See Wafer, J., 1982 for more information on the Warlpiri kinship system.

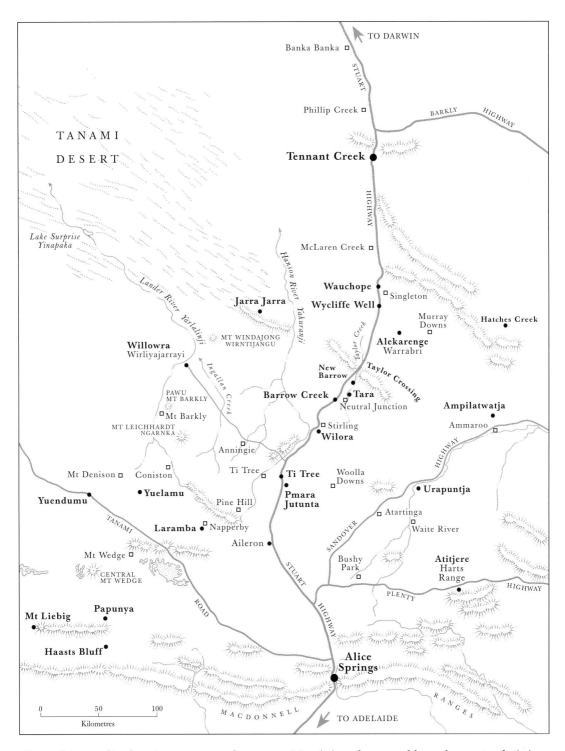

Central Australia showing towns and communities (•) and pastoral lease homesteads (□).

For a list of alternative placenames, see the map *Current Distribution of Central Australian Languages* (IAD, 1990).

Yarla — bush yam by Violet Nampijinpa Downs. Linocut print, 1993

Part One

Following the tracks of our ancestors: living from country

We hold our country eternally

Molly Nungarrayi and Lady Nampijinpa, in their capacity as senior women at Willowra, began their oral histories with these introductory speeches. By citing personal links to ancestors, Jukurrpa (Dreamings) and country, Nungarrayi and Nampijinpa establish their social identity and thus their right to tell the stories which take place in the Lander River region. They then discuss who is going to talk first, and why. Nungarrayi explains that her authority to talk derives from a lifetime of learning about her country from a generation of people who have now passed away, and that the Jukurrpa she follows is not of recent origin. It has always existed and will exist forever. Lucy Nampijinpa, a middle-aged woman, then explains that it is appropriate for the older women to speak first.

Georgina Napangardi (centre rear) recording her mothers-in-law Rosie Nungarrayi (left) and Molly Nungarrayi (right) telling stories under a bough shade while little Nangala (their granddaughter) looks on, 1988.

Molly Nungarrayi

WARLPIRI	*STANDARD ENGLISH*
Nyurruwiyi kalarnalu nyinaja nyampurla, ngajuku-palangu jamirdi-kirli manu jaja-kurlu kula nguru-karirla nyampurla yantarli. Ngajuku-palangu kirdana manu ngati kalapala nyinaja nyampurla, manu warru wapaja nyampurla kula nguru-karirla. Wiri-jarrijarna ngajuku-palangu-parnta nyampurla yantarli. Warlalja	In the olden days we lived here, with my grandfather and grandmother — not at other places, but here. My father and mother lived here, and walked around here — not other places. I grew up here with my grandmother in one place. My family doesn't belong anywhere else but strictly to this country. My children are from here,

ngajuku-palangu-patu kula kalu nyina nguru-kari-wardingki. Lawa nyampuku yantarliki kalu nyinami. Kurdu-kurdu ngaju-nyangu kalu nyina nyampu-wardingki, manu kalu nyina wiri ngatijirriki manu wawirriki jukurrpaku ngajuku-palangu-kurlanguku.

Muturna-muturna-kurlangu yimi kula kamina-kamina-kurlangu. Ngaju-nyangu jukurrpaju tarnngajuku. Purami karnalu jukurrpaju yimiji jamirdi-nyanungurlu manu jaja-nyanungurlu, manu ngati-ngirli, manu kirdana-ngurlu. Ngulanya karnalu-nyanu warra-warra-kanyi nguruju. Mardarni karnalu-nyanu yimiji pirrjirdirli.

Lawa-jarrijalu nganimpaku-palangu-patuju kulalpalu yanurnu Ngarnalkurru-ngurlu, Patirlirri-ngirli manu Yinapaka-ngurlu Liirlpari-kirra manu Murranjayi-kirra. Kalarnalu wungujuku wapaja nguru nganimpa-nyangu-wanaju Japanangka manu Japaljarri-kurlangu.

Japanangka-kurlangu-patulu wirijarrija warlalja-patuju Napangardi-kurlangu manu Nungarrayi-kurlangu manu Jungarrayi purdangka-kurlangu kurdu-kurdu. Japanangka-kurlangu warlalja. Ngarrurnu-palunganpa kurdu-kurdu, manu karnalu milya-pinyi nyiya-kanti-kantiji nganimpaku-palangu-ngurluju. Nganimpaku-palangurlu kalu-nganpa pina-yinyi. Nyanyi karnalu-jana manu karnalu manngi-nyanyi nyurruwiyi-warnu-kurluju.

Nganimpaku-palangu-paturlu kujalu nganpa milki-yungu. Mardarni-karnalu Law nganimpa-nyangu tarnngangkujuku. ❑

from the Budgerigar and Kangaroo Jukurrpa of my father.

Old women's Law. Not young women. My Jukurrpa is eternal.[1] We are following the Jukurrpa stories from our grandmothers and grandfathers, mothers and fathers. That's why we have to look after the country. We are keeping the Law strong.[2]

Our people passed away while they were travelling from Ngarnalkurru, Patirlirri and Yinapaka to Liirlpari and Muranjayi. We used to all walk together all over the land to our in-laws' country, that of Japanangka and Japaljarri.

Japanangka's family grew bigger, with the birth of Napangardi [daughter] and Nungarrayi and Jungarrayi [sister's daughter's children]. A lot of family for Japanangka. They called us children, and we still know everything from our grandparents. Our grandfather used to teach us. We watched them and we still remember from a long time ago. Our grandparents showed us when we were children and we understand everything now because we were well educated. From the time that we were little children we learnt things, right up until we grew big and became old. It was as a child that I began to learn and carry it on.

We are still holding it, we are still looking after it. Our understanding continues forever. We keep the Law eternally. ❑

---

[1] Here 'eternal' is a translation of the Warlpiri *tarnnga*, meaning 'forever', 'always'.
[2] Warlpiri Law from the Jukurrpa.

Lady Nampijinpa

WARLPIRI	STANDARD ENGLISH

Ngajuku-palangu kirdanaju Pawu-wardingki, manu ngaju-nyangu warringiyi. Ngajurna wirijarrija yalirlajuku, manu ngajuku-palangu ngamirdi-kirlangurla. Kularna wapaja wurnturu wurnturu nyinajalparna ngajuku-palangu kurlangurla ngurrararla. Ngajurna palka-jarrija manurna ngarnu ngamirdi-kirlangu ngatijirri jukurrpa. Ngajurna ngarnu ngapurlu ngaju nyangu ngamirdi-kirlangu ngatijirri. Ngajurna ngulaju Pawu-wardingki. Ngaju nyangu ngamardiki purdangkapatu ngulaju nyampujuku palka. Ngajujurna ngulaju Pawu-wardingki ngulanya karna wangkami manu ngarrirni yimi nyampurraju. ❐

My father belongs to Mount Barkly, and my grandfather. I grew up there, and at the place belonging to my mother. I didn't travel far away but stayed near my country. I was born there and drank from my mother of the Budgerigar Jukurrpa. I drank the milk from my mother, the Budgerigar. My mother's three sisters are all here. I'm from the Mount Barkly country, this is why I'm speaking and telling these stories. ❐

Janet Nakamarra (front) making a 'mud map' of sites mentioned by women in their accounts, while Lucy Nampijinpa leafs through photos taken during the Willowra land claim, 1988.

Lucy Nampijinpa

WARLPIRI	STANDARD ENGLISH

Ngaju karna wangkami muturna muturna kurlu, ngajuku palangu ngamardi-patu manu pimirdi-patu kurlu manu nyarrparlu kuja kalalu ngarrurnu yimi nyurruwarnu-patu manu yapa-kurlangu kuruwarri. Nampijinpa-warnurlu kapurlu kanyi kuruwarri muturna muturna-warnu-kurlangu. Muturna muturnarla kapulu-ngalpa jiilyngarrirni ngana yungu Nampijinpa wangkami, kuja kalalu ngalpa warru-kangu kurdu kurduwiyi, kujala ngalpa palkamanu ngalipa. Nganimpa nyangu ngamirdirli Nungarrayi-patu wirrkardurlu kalalu nganpa yungu ngurlu ngurrara-jangka. Ngajulu kapurna jana ngarrirni yimi muturna muturna-piyarlu. ❐

I'm talking about the old women, my mothers and aunties, and how they are telling stories about the olden days, about Aboriginal Law. The Nampijinpas [daughters] are going to follow the old women. The old women are responsible for choosing which of us Nampijinpas will also talk, because they carried us around as children. They gave birth to us. Our mothers, the three Nungarrayis, nourished us with seed from the country. I'll be telling stories like those women. ❐

Hunting and gathering

Before European contact, Lander Warlpiri led a hunter-gatherer existence: women hunted small animals and gathered vegetable food, while men hunted larger animals like kangaroo, turkey and emu. Although many aspects of the lifestyle changed after white settlement, hunting and gathering continued to form the basis of the Aboriginal economy until the 1950s. Over the years, feral animals such as rabbits and cats were added to the diet, and rifles, axes and other new technologies were adopted where available. Today, as a result of livestock grazing, the onslaught of feral animals, and changed fire management practices,[1] many of the small mammals that the women once caught are no longer around in large numbers, if at all. Yet, despite the deterioration in the local ecology, bush food is still much desired, and people hunt and gather whenever the opportunity arises.

The spiritual benefits of obtaining food from the country are as important to people as the taste. The practice of hunting and gathering is not just an economic activity but involves an embodied relationship with the land. Different areas of land or 'country' are identified with different groups of people who believe themselves to be descended from the Jukurrpa beings who created the particular landscape. When Warlpiri travel around the land they point out the trees, rockholes, and natural features where ancestral activities occurred. These sites are named places on the landscape. A person's country is thought of as being the area surrounding the sites which lie along the travel routes or 'tracks' made by that person's Jukurrpa ancestor. It is a person's spiritual link with the land that confers the rights to use the economic resources of, and live on, that land. As well as the right to use the resources, the 'owners' of the land have the responsibility to care for the land. They do so through the performance of ceremonies and by actively engaging with the country through activities such as hunting and gathering.

In the following stories, Molly and Rosie (Ruth) describe how people lived in the Lander River area, hunting and gathering during the first half of this century. The Lander River area borders the Tanami Desert and thus is hot and arid: in summer, temperatures during the day regularly soar to forty degrees or more, and winter nights can drop to zero. In the past, the availability of water and the two main seasons of summer and winter governed the pattern of hunting.[2] Most rain falls in the summer, when the Lander River flows from bank to bank for a brief period, and the rockholes and claypans fill up. After a few months the river dries up, leaving soakages in the river bed. During the dry season, people relied on natural springs and on soakages in the Lander to obtain water. Their intimate knowledge of the country, of the varied landscapes and different flora and fauna, meant that they could obtain sufficient water and a varied diet throughout the year.

As recounted by Molly and Rosie, people travelled around in small groups of one or two families, and as they walked from place to place they met up with relatives along the way. In good seasons when there was much rain, a number of families would gather together to hold ceremonies and enjoy social intercourse. As children walked through the country with

---

[1] Pastoralists discouraged the Aboriginal practice of firing the country to control and promote the growth of vegetation, and, as a result, the flora and fauna have changed significantly.

[2] In accordance with Warlpiri usage, from here on the term 'hunting' will be used to refer to both hunting and gathering, of food and other resources.

their parents, they learnt how to recognise animal tracks and how to hunt. They came to know the features of the landscape intimately and began learning Jukurrpa stories about life and the land. The social and economic aspects of Warlpiri society were thus integrated with religion in a very personal way.

Rosie Nungarrayi

In the olden time we walked around hunting, catching goannas, gathering berries, and digging for yams. We'd track down wild cats and catch them and we'd kill lizards and goannas. The animals gathered at the big soakages and we'd go there to catch them. We travelled to Mount Barkly from Patirlirri, and from Patirlirri we walked to Liirlpari. At Liirlpari we caught rabbits, wild cats and bandicoots. No whiteman's flour — only food from the land. After Liirlpari we went to Wirliyajarrayi. We stopped overnight at soakages and caught rabbits along the creek.

In the Jukurrpa an emu came travelling to Wirliyajarrayi from the south, where he had been speared. At Wirliyajarrayi he was speared again. This is the Jukurrpa.

After Wirliyajarrayi we went to Kunarurrpa, another soakage.

We travelled along the Yarlalinji [Lander River], eating acacia seeds and collecting *yaka-jirri* raisins and *wakirlpirri* beans. We'd grow thirsty out hunting and return to the soakage for water. On the way back we ate rabbit and wild cat, and sometimes dingo. Then we'd eat seeds, *yakajirri* raisins, yams, and goanna. No flour. We lived on bush food. This is how we were grown up by our fathers and mothers and grandparents. ❐

Mayleen Nampijinpa holds Gwendolyn Nangala/Napurrula up to the tree to listen for the buzz of bees making honey.

Molly Nungarrayi

My father used to look around for meat. He'd find some and kill it, then he'd keep walking, looking for more. He'd find more meat — meat from bush animals. He'd look around and find goanna tracks. Then he'd follow them to a hole and start digging until he found the goanna. He used to go out hunting from a bough shade and after hunting he'd go back to that same shade, bringing lots of meat. My mother would wait there for him with vegetable food and water. Then she'd see him coming carrying meat. He'd come and sit down and pour water over himself to cool off. Then my mother would make a fire and start cooking. My father had meat for his wife, some for his parents, and some for his mother- and father-in-law.

When the sun went down they were ready to go back to the camp, where others waited for them to bring meat. The mother used to look out for her daughter, and the father watched for his son coming back home. Then the father would go over to his son's camp to get meat. The father gave seeds, *yakajirri* raisins, wild tomatoes and yams to his son, in exchange for meat, which he took home for his wife. Then they'd eat some of their son's meat and share the rest with other people. The father would give some of his son's meat to his daughter who lived at the single women's camp, and he also gave some to his wife's parents. They shared the bush meat with their relatives. That's how they grew strong and healthy — from bush meat. That was in the olden time.

They used to share meat such as *pakuru* [bandicoot], *purdujurru* [brush-tailed bettong],

Left: Gathering jurlarda *(bush honey), 1987. Having just cut down a branch which contains* jurlarda, *Leah Nampijinpa watches while the women scoop the honey into containers.*
Top right: Nampijinpa with a bark dish containing jurlarda.
Lower right: Close up of jurlarda *lying in the centre of a branch.*

mala [rufous hare-wallaby], *wawirri* [plains kangaroo], and *yankirri* [emu]. They'd spear the animals while they were lying in the shade. Then they'd share the meat with other family members: mothers, mother's father and mother's mother and others. This was a long time ago, in the olden days. Nowadays they do the same for us. Our grandsons and granddaughters do that — as in the olden days, when they shared meat with each other. They looked after each other and old people properly, dear things. ❐

Molly Nungarrayi

We started off walking from one soakage and followed goanna tracks. I sang out, 'Let me dig for it,' and I dug the goanna out and put it on the winnowing dish. Then we headed off again, looking for honey. I sang out, 'Let me cut the tree,' and I cut out the honey from the branch of a tree and filled the bark container. Later we found a yam bush. 'Let us dig for yams,' I said. We dug, dug and dug. Then, when the bark container was full, we walked off. We'd find yams by looking for cracks in the ground. We dug really big yams and then walked off again. Then, after walking some more, we found goanna tracks and followed them. We dug one hole and then saw that the goanna had left for another hole, so we followed it. We used to take dogs with us to follow the goanna tracks. They'd sniff the goanna out and chase it around until it fled up a tree. We'd run after it and throw sticks at it until it fell out and we caught it.

While travelling from place to place we got lots of food. We found vegetable food and dug for it. Then we said, 'The containers are all full now. It's getting a bit hot, so we should go and look for water.' On the way to a soakage we found goanna or wild cat tracks. In the heat of the day a wild cat runs along trying to find shade to lie in. The dogs would smell it and go straight to it, chasing the wild cat until it climbed the tree. Then we'd kill the cat and get the guts out.

On coming to a soakage we'd look around for a good spot to sit in the shade. 'Which one [tree] is a good place to sit? Maybe this one.' Then we looked for water and took it back to the shade where we'd sit. After the rain there was always lots of water. Later we lit a fire and cooked the meat. We ate some and saved a bit over for later, leaving the meat on a branch. Then we rested in the shade until late afternoon, when we went out hunting again.

We made our camp there at that shady place and, at night, we returned to it with all our food. After hunting we cooked and ate the food. We left some for later and then went to sleep. We only stayed at that place for one night, or perhaps for two nights, then we said, 'Let's go and look for tracks of people.' We walked to another soakage, digging yams and hunting all the way. We got lots of different types of yams and then said, 'We have to go and look for water.' On the way to the soakage we saw tracks. 'There were people living here the day before yesterday,' we said. There was a bough shade belonging to other people who had stayed here earlier. 'They must be at another soakage,' we said. It was true.

We stayed there and cooked our food. We said to each other, 'In the afternoon we have to go and look for those people who were here.' Later in the afternoon we had dinner and got ready to go to another soakage. As we walked along we saw grass burning from other people's fires, and then we saw their bough shade and camp. 'They left here yesterday, maybe they are staying over at the next soakage,' we said. We followed them, on and on, and then we saw another bush fire.

Those other people had said to each other, 'Oh, there must be people coming today.' One woman had felt twitches. She had a funny feeling in her arm and she told the rest that maybe people were coming. Then she stood up and looked around everywhere and saw some people coming a long way in the distance. 'The other group is coming, there are lots of people coming,' she said. Then she recognised them. 'Oh, it's them. That's my family coming. My mother and father, and my uncle and my grandmother.' She ran towards them. Then she ran back to tell the others that the people were approaching. They sat together waiting for the others to come closer. Then the people greeted each other. 'We saw your tracks and then we followed them,' we said to them. They gave us some meat and water because we'd walked a long way. Later in the afternoon they made windbreaks for us, then we all slept. They made bough shades for us and we stayed there, living together for a long time.

We'd go out hunting in the mornings for food. We'd go in different directions from the soakage, spearing meat, spearing kangaroo while it rested in the shade. Others speared emus that were drinking at the soakage. They dragged them away from the soakage, then cleaned the intestines out and cooked them. When an emu was cooked they took it out of the fire, cut it into pieces, and carried it back to the camp. A woman would see her husband coming back from hunting with lots of meat and she'd say to the others, 'He's got the meat, we can all share it.' The man would sit in the shade and share the meat with everyone. He'd give it to his fathers, mothers, grandmothers and grandfathers, and to the women in the single women's camp. They used to share the meat with the single women.

They stayed there for a long time, going out hunting for food. Later, maybe one week later, they'd go to a different place to camp. There they'd get yams, berries and seeds. Then the cold weather would come and there was much rain. When we had this big rain we had lots of bush food, as I just said. After the rain all the bush food came out. There were things growing like *yakajirri* raisins and different types of seeds. They used to collect bush food and winnow it in a dish. Then they'd make the seeds into a seed cake. They used to get different types of seeds around Patirlirri and Jirringipinki. They'd grind the seeds and make them into seed cakes. This happened around this area.

Topsy Nangala with **kanta** *(bush coconuts), a billy-can of* **wanakiji** *(bush tomatoes) and a crowbar for a digging stick.*

We didn't have flour bags in the olden time. We'd sew bits of old blankets together to make a seed bag. Our parents used to winnow different seeds like *warrapinyi, lukarrara, kirdawarri, wakati, warnararlpa* and *munyuparntiparnti*. The old men used to go out hunting. They'd dig yams and put them in bark containers. They'd kill goannas and bring them home, and they'd bring back other animals such as *mala* [rufous hare-wallaby], *purdujurru* [brush-tailed bettong] and *yarrkamardi* [brush-tailed bettong]. When they came back home their wives and children met them. Our fathers brought home meat and shared it with our grandparents, our mothers and our older sisters. ❐

10

Keeping track of family

Molly Nungarrayi

We moved to another place and looked for other people on the way. We lit fires to signal that we were coming. 'Let's go and look for the others. Maybe someone is sick,' we said. Then two men went looking for their father, who was at another soakage. They took one day to get to there, and when they arrived they said to the old man, 'We came for you, we thought you might be sick.' 'I'm all right,' he answered. 'We were worried about you,' they told the old man again, 'We will take you back home with us.'

One man said to the other, 'You take them straight back home while I go and look for meat.' So the son-in-law walked by his parents-in-law's side as their son looked for meat. They walked into camp together, taking meat with them. 'Here they come,' everyone said. Then the people in the camp gave seeds, yams and other food to the visitors. They fed them because they were tired from walking. The visitors said, 'The place where we lit signals for you lot, that was the soakage where we were staying.' Then they told each other their news: 'I saw lots of yams to the north. We might go there because I saw lots of food there.' ❐

Yinarlingi *(spiny anteater, or echidna) is highly prized meat.*

Ceremony: following the Jukurrpa

Lucy Nampijinpa leads Willowra dancers performing Pawu Jukurrpa during Yuendumu Sports weekend, 1991.

Jukurrpa, or Dreaming as it is called in English, is the creation period of the Warlpiri; the time when ancestral beings travelled the land and performed creative acts which gave substance and meaning to the world. Every Warlpiri person is descended from particular ancestral Jukurrpa beings and associated with the country that was given shape by those ancestral beings.

In order to ensure the well-being and continuity of people and the land, Warlpiri are expected to fulfil ritual responsibilities according to the Law of the Jukurrpa. Both men and women have religious responsibilities but, while they share a body of knowledge about Jukurrpa, there are important areas of difference. A major part of men's religious life is secret, and neither women nor children have access to it. Women also have a rich religious life. They perform ceremonies called **yawulyu,** *which enact the travels of ancestral beings over the land. The yawulyu songs, dances and paintings of ancestral designs encode information about a woman's Jukurrpa and the countries to which she belongs. Through the performance of ceremonies, women's associations with country are strengthened, as are the social bonds between the people linked to these countries. Ceremonies also mark significant cultural transitions in a person's life. Boys, for example, must be initiated in order to become accepted into Warlpiri society as men.*

Here Molly Nungarrayi and Nampijinpa recount how they watched yawulyu performances when they were young girls. Nungarrayi then describes how different families gathered together for initiation ceremonies.

Molly Nungarrayi

My two sisters and I and Molly Napangardi's family, from Ngarnalkurru, performed *yawulyu* in the olden time. True. When I was a young girl we watched our families singing and dancing. They used to paint the women's sacred designs on their bodies and sing the Jukurrpa songs for the countries Yinjirrpi-kirlangu and Ngarnalkurru. They'd follow the Jukurrpa north to Rdapurdu. They danced and sang in the way that we do these days.

The olden time ceremonies belonged to Japaljarri and Japanangka and to Napangardi and Napurrula. Those olden time Jukurrpa were dear ones.[1] We used to watch those women's ceremonies. They used to sing Jukurrpa songs starting from Mawukurlangu and Ngarnalkurru. This country belongs to Japaljarri, Napaljarri, Japanangka, Napanangka, to Jungarrayi and Nungarrayi and to Napangardi and Japangardi. Many people from Ngarnalkurru used to dance. We watched these ceremonies when we were young girls. The

---

[1] Cherished, sacred.

owners of the land used to walk around their country singing their Jukurrpa songs. ❐

Nampijinpa

I watched them dig yams and then dance in the olden time. When we were young girls we saw them dancing. They were painted with designs and danced at night time, all the Nakamarras, Napurrulas, Napangardis, Nampijinpas and Nungarrayis. They made the children go to sleep, and the old ladies danced all night. In the daytime they went away from the camp to hunt and to dance without the kids watching. Mothers went for the dancing and came back to camp in the afternoon. Those Nakamarras and Nangalas who danced at Ngarnalkurru and who ground seeds in the south camp, they have all passed away. They provided seed cakes for their sons-in-law in the single men's camps and for married couples and their children.[2] ❐

In full swing: Kathy Nangala and Topsy Nangala recreate the travels of their Jukurrpa ancestors across the Pawu landscape, 1977.

Nungarrayi

People would come from other places to the soakage where the initiation ceremony was to be held. They'd send one man to gather up people from other places. They'd gather up family from Yurrkuru and Ngarningirri.[3] My uncle lived in that area and he used to hold ceremonies for his relatives.

Japanangka and Japaljarri used to wait for everyone to come up here for the ceremony. As I said, Jupurrula and Jakamarra used to come from Ngarningirri and Yurrkuru. They'd all meet up and dance for the country at Pirliwanawana. People also came to Willowra from Ngarnalkurru. Our family, from Wirliyajarrayi and Ngarnalkurru. They met in large groups in one place. Japanangkas from Warlukurlangu also came. They used to follow their own Jukurrpa and put the Jukurrpa designs on their bodies. Our grandparents followed the Jukurrpa which came to Willowra. Patirlirri is still an important place for ceremony. The business goes on and on forever. ❐

---

[2] At the time we recorded the women talking about yawulyu ceremonies, Johnny Japaljarri Kitson recounted his memories of women performing yawulyu as follows: 'I'm Japaljarri, talking at Willowra. I'm telling you about the early days, the way people used to live. When they wanted to have business the old women were really hard and strong. They didn't dance close to the camps, they went a long way away. Their ceremonies were too hard. In the daytime they went out quietly, maybe two miles away, and they danced until late at night. All the old women went dancing, leaving the children behind, because they were too young to go to these ceremonies. When they came back home, all the young girls saw them wearing yawulyu designs. I knew about this dancing because I saw this happen when I was a young boy. They came back later. When the sun went down and the kids were asleep, the ladies began to dance at the camp. They used to light fires and sing and dance in the night time. That was how it happened. They were really strong.'

[3] These sites are on Mount Denison Station.

Health: looking after each other

Here Nungarrayi describes how people looked after each other in the 'old days'. By properly observing the rights and responsibilities particular kin had towards each other, the social health of the group was maintained. When individuals became sick, bush medicines — plants with medicinal properties — were used to cure the illness.

Molly Nungarrayi

In the olden days they looked after each other, in the olden time. Poor things, the old people — grandmothers, grandfathers, fathers and mothers — used to look after each other. They didn't rubbish each other. Our daughters looked after us also. The people looked after a kinsman until he grew older and older and became sick and tired and passed away. Then they buried him. All the deceased's relatives did this, women and men. They used to get firewood for the old people and make windbreaks and humpies in case it rained. The younger ones kept on looking after those poor old things, because the old ones once got food for them and took care of them. The old men fed us young ones from the time that they were single until they were married.

Nangala with **wardapi** *(sand monitor)*

When grandma was sick her husband found bush medicine for her. When there were bad colds everyone got them — even the old ones. The old man made bush medicine for them and made them better. When everyone was healthy again the husband went off hunting, and the mother and daughter looked for goannas, yams and seeds.

When we were sick they gathered medicine from the bush and used it to cure our sickness. When we had colds they rubbed us with this bush medicine and put the plant in our nose so that we could inhale it. There was no whitefella medicine. They used to rub the medicine everywhere, all over our bodies. The next morning the person used to wake up feeling good and well. That's how they made us better, with bush medicine. Before whitefella medicine or motorcars. ❐

Giving birth using bush medicine

Here Nungarrayi looks back to the time when women gave birth out bush and people were healthy. She describes the practice in which the mother and baby are smoked after a birth — a ritual that continues to be observed today. The process involves the grandmother placing the baby and mother in the smoke of branches of cassia bushes and supplejack, which are smouldering in a hole filled with embers and crushed antbed. Both mother and baby are rubbed with crushed antbed, and a small amount of the substance is placed in the baby's mouth.

Molly Nungarrayi

WARLPIRI	STANDARD ENGLISH

Yarlungka, yarlungka karnalu ngurrju nyina lawa walyka-karirla purraku, purrakurla walykangka yupujurla-ju. Yirnalu ngarni purraku, wurrkuparrirni yinga-rnalu-nyanu warririrli yulpayirlarlu, yungkiyi yinga-rnalu wurrkuparrirni. Kunjururlalpa purraja, mingkirrilparla jankajarni, watu-watulparlajinta jankajarni. Ngati-nyanurlulpa kilyirrparlu purrajarni kurdulpa purrajarni, ngula-purupalurla puyu pungurnu mingkirri. Ngati-nyanuku kurdukulpalu-jana wungu-jarraku, yungu mingkirriji puyu-pinjarla manulpalu-jana maparnu mingkirri-kirlirliji. Ngati-nyanululpa-nyanu nyampu palka jingi-jingi maparnu ngapurlupinki ngarninjaku pirrjirdi karda kurduku nyanungurlulpa ngarnu-ngatinyanurlu ngulangku wiyijuku yupuju-ngawurrparlu wiri-manu nyampuju kurdu.

Ngula ka lirri-nyina nganimpa-nyangu wati kurdukupalangu panuku-palangulku kula walypalijangka wijipitirli-jangka, lawa yupuju-warnu ka lirri-nyina ngulajulparnalu-jana yupuju-wanajuku wanka manu rdakurl-yirrarnu. No doctor, lawa, manangkarrajangkajuku yilparnalu-jana nyampurlarlu rdakurl-rdakurl-yirrarnu.

Palka-jarrijalpalu nyampukula warrikirdi-kirdi. Kulalparnalurla walypaliki doctor wangkaja, lawa, juulmarlijukulpa kurdungka jintajulpa yawuru-jarrija ngulajuku, ngakalpa palkalku pipakurra-manulpa, nyangulpa

We used to live out in the bush, where it was cooler and there was good fresh water. The water was fresh and good to drink and to wash with. When pregnant women felt pain, they knew that the baby was ready to be born. They used to give birth out in the bush, where wood was plentiful and they could smoke both the baby and the mother. They would collect antbed to use as a rubbing medicine. They rubbed their bodies all over, and they also drank a mixture of antbed and water in order to become strong and healthy. That's how we cared for our children a long time ago. Those children are now adults and living here with their children.

There was never a white doctor around to help us with our babies. We never went to the clinic to see the sister. No, we had our babies just out in the bush, with some other women helping us.

They were born here — in this country. We did not tell the white doctors, but had our children out bush. Later, after our babies were stronger, we would take them to the sister, who would give them names

wirilki ngulawarnujuku ka nyampuju lirri-nyina nganimpanyangu wirriya, mardukuja panukirda, panuku-palangu yupuju-warnujuku. Yupuju-ngkajukulu palka-jarrinjarla muku wiri-jarrija. Nyampu jalangu-warnupatu ngulaju nyanguwaji ngawurrpalku, wijipitirli-ngawurrpalku nyampuju, kala ngulaju nyurruwarnu-patu luwungkawiyi ngulajulparnalujana muku wanka-yirrarnu ngurrjunyayirni, lawa.

Ya parrajarla kalarnalujana mukurnu-yirrarnu. Jalangu-warnu-patuju panja yangka kalarnalu-jana kujurnu wawarda yangka warlalja-nyayirni nyampurlaju. Jalangu-jalanguju ngulaju walypali ngaanjirrilki ngulalu nyampurla palka-jarrija muku kurdu-kurdu nguru nyampurla jalanguju, nyurruwiyi ngulaju parraja kalarlujana jarnturnu. Parrajarla kalarnalujana purlakitirla palkajuku mukurnu-mukurnu-yirrarnu, panja-panja-yirrarnu. Nguru nyampurla ngulangkanya kalarnalu-jana wiri-wiri milki-yirrarnu yalumpurrakurrakula.

Ngajarrarlu-jana Lady-jarra Lucy-jarra, milki-kangulurla wiri-wirilkijiki lawa nyurru. Ngulawarnuju kalu ngurrju-nyina. kula kalalu nyurnu-wantija yupuju-wanajangka, ngurra-wana-jangka yarrkujuju-wana-jangka, walku, jalanguju walypalijangka, nyanguwaji-jangka, rdakawarnu ngula-warnulku jalpi. Kala yupuju-wana-jangka ngulaju pijirrdi kalu nyina, wiri-jarrijalu. Jungajuku-rnalujana wijipitirli-kirra kangu ngurra-jangka, yupuju-wana-jangka, juulmarlujangka, pirrjirdi.

and then write the names on a record chart. That's how our children were raised around this country. Those children who were born and raised in the bush are now grown and have children themselves. Nowadays pregnant women go to the clinics and hospitals, but in the olden days their children were born in the bush and raised according to the Law, and it was good.

We carried our newborn children around in coolamons softened with blankets, and only later did we show them to the sisters. I remember showing Lady and Lucy when they were older. They were strong and healthy for having been born in the bush. These days children are all delivered into the doctors' hands in the smelly hospitals. Sometimes, when the children go home from hospital with their mothers, they become sick and have to fly back to the hospitals again. When they were born out bush away from everyone they were strong and healthy.

Termite mounds dot the landscape to the north-east of Wirliyajarrayi. Antbed such as this is used as a rubbing medicine for mother and child after childbirth.

Kala nyanguwajirli ngula ka wanka-wanka-yirrarni kurdu-kurdu yangka pukulyurlalku yinya wijipitirla-rlalku wiringka ngula-warnuju ka murru-murru pina pardimirra pardimirra yaliwarnu murru-murrulkujuku. Kala nyampurla ngulalparnalujana wiri-wiri manu yupuju-wana, ngulaju murru-murruwangu, lawa. Kalarnalu wapajarra-wapajarra nyampukula parrajakurlu, parraja-kurlu, ya, yupuju-wardingki mangarri mirrijini yalirlinya kalarnalujana wurrkuparrurni manu yungu kalarnalu-jana. Ngarnu kalalu yupuju-wardingki mangarri wurrkuparrarni manu kalarnalu-jana jungarrayi-jungarrayirli, mirrijirni-wangurluku. Ngulangku kalarnalu-jana ngurrju-manu mirrijini-wangurlawiyiji kurdu-kurdu nyampu. Ngula kalu matirini wirriya, mardukuja lawa. Kalarnalu-jana pirrjirdi ngurrju-manu bush medicine-rlijuku. Wiri-jarrijalu murru-murruwangujuku. ❐

Everywhere today babies are born with all sorts of sickness, or there is always something wrong with them. Before, when we had our babies, they were born strong, with no sickness. When we went out hunting for bush food or medicine, we would carry them around in the coolamons, where they slept comfortably. When we washed our babies we would mix *jungarrayi-jungarrayi* [a plant with medicinal properties] with water to keep them strong. Before white man's medicine our babies grew up strong, with no sickness. They grew into the adults that they are now, living here with their wives and children. ❐

Nampijinpa digs for **yarla** *(yams).*

Childhood: how they grew us up

Here Nangala describes how she grew up eating different types of bush food. She recalls waiting in the camp for her father and grandfather to come home with the kill from the day's hunt. In the mornings she was often surprised with hare-wallaby or possum meat that had been caught during the night.

Topsy Nangala

My grandfather used to go out hunting and spear emus. (He died later, at the time the army was here.) He used to spear a lot of animals in this area. When I was a small child they fed me with berries like *marnikiji, yakajirri, yipirntiri, yankurlayi* and *wanakiji* [bush tomatoes]. That's how they grew us up. When we started walking we ate these things, and also when we were children playing around. We used to make little seed carriers with the bark of the river red gum trees. 'There comes my grandfather with an emu from out hunting. Let me run to him,' I'd say. I used to eat his meat. My father stopped us from eating too much. He'd say, 'Oh, you children, go away, don't eat too much or you'll get diarrhoea, go away.' But while he was saying this we'd be walking off eating meat, and eating *marnikiji* [bush sultanas] and *yakajirri* berries. That's how they grew us up.

When we were children we ate everything, the food that belonged to the olden time people. We ate bush food at Ngarnalkurru. 'There come our mother and our two grandmothers. They're back from hunting,' we'd call out to each other. We'd run to them, happy. We'd eat meat and then go to sleep. In the morning they'd go off again and get more meat and bush food. At night, when the moon was high, they hunted *wampana* [spectacled hare-wallaby]. We children would be asleep and didn't know what was happening. The next morning we'd wake up and see lots of possum and wampana everywhere. This happened at Yakuranji, on the Hanson River, and also around the Willowra area.

Topsy Nangala with her **warringiyi** *(grandson – Petronella Vaarzon-Morel's son), Marcelis Avery, 1994.*

Two Nungarrayis with baby kangaroo.

Our mothers and fathers used to tell us to take some meat to eat and go and play. I ate my mother's and grandmother's food. My grandmother and mother used to go out hunting, and we'd stay at home, eating their food. 'Let me go and get my grandfather's meat,' I'd say. I used to run home and get my grandfather's or father's meat and bring it back to where the other children were playing. Once the kids hit me, saying, 'Give us some meat.' I cried, 'You mob go and get your own, I went to my grandfather's place and got this for myself.'

I used to wake up from sleeping in the afternoon and then sit, sit, sit, waiting for my grandmothers. My grandfather speared kangaroo and brought the meat back in a bark carrier. Oh, everything he brought, goanna and honey. I told my two grandmothers that the other kids were hitting me for my meat. My grandmother spoke to them in Kaytetye, saying, 'Don't you fight with her any more, leave her alone, she's only little.' ❐

A tree burial

In this story Nungarrayi describes the traditional burial of her grandfather, who died as a result of a curse placed on him by a relative. The deceased's body was laid on a mortuary platform placed in a tree. Nungarrayi's family mourned her grandfather in the traditional way, which involves persons inflicting wounds upon themselves to show the depth of their sorrow.

Rosie Nungarrayi

WARLPIRI	STANDARD ENGLISH
Wapajarnalu-uu kakarrapurda-yijala, nyampu Yakuranji-kirra. Yatijarra-purdarnalu yanu, yatijarra-purdalku wapaja kulkurru wiyijiki. Yakuranjirla. Yakuranjirla-wardinkgirla-jarrija, wakirlpirri-payirla-jarrija, ngurlungka-jarrija, yakajirrirla-jarrija ngurrju-parntawiyijiki jaja-kariparnta jinta-kari-parnta nganimpaku-palangu-parnta-aa. Wapanja-yanu-mpa yaa wiri-jarlu, yuwa kajika-palanyanu warlamarra-manilki. Ngari yangka nyampu ngari nyinanya nyiya mayi Ngirriliya Nampijinpa? Kujanya yali-nyarnalu pardijarni jurrkukurrayijala nyampukurra warlamarra-kurlulku nyurdukurlulku jaja-wangukari-kirliji. Yanurnurnalu, yuwa.	We travelled east again, to Yakuranji [Hanson Creek]. We went northwards, we walked north for a while. At Yakuranji we were happy. We found *wakirlpirri* beans and *yakajirri* [bush raisins] there. A lot of people were travelling around. During that time my grandparents, who walked together, cursed each other. In fact, the one who is the widow — who is it? Oh, Ngirriliya Nampijinpa, yes, she is the one who is the widow. My grandfather, who passed away at that time, was the husband of Ngirriliya. From there we set out for the same place again with the one who had been cursed and was sick. They carried my grandfather on their shoulders. Yes, we came in.
Ngarnalkurru-wardingkirla yangka nguru-kurra jurrku-kurrarnalu pinarni jurduly-wantija. Ngulaju wungujuku malirlangu-jarraju, jurdalja, wajamirni wurdu-wurdu nyiya Yakuranji-ngirli nyampungurlunya. Ngula ka Yakuranji yangka nguna Hanson Creek ngulawana. Yanurnurnalu-nyurdukurlu, nyurdukurlu, nyurdukurlu, nyurdukurlu, nyurdukurlu, nyurdukurlu, warlamarrakurluju. 'Jurrkukurra nganta yarujuyawu!' Warriripiya-kurra nyampukurraju, yuwa, kujarnikirla nyampu Jarra-jarra-kurrapinangu. Yuwa. Jarrajarrakurra-pinangu. Ngayarrkamardipinki, yalirra. Ngulajukunya yilparnalu juul-juul-nyinaja w a p a n j a - p a r n t a - k u r l u w i y i jajawangukurluju.	In the hot weather we travelled with my grandfather to the homeland of Ngarnal-kurru. We travelled on and turned back again to the same country. We travelled to the same place with our sons-in-law and their family, from Yakuranji on the Hanson Creek, carrying the one who was sick from the curse. We travelled back to a place not far from here, yes, in this direction, and then back to Jarrajarra, then over there to places associated with Ngayarrkamara. We rested there with my grandfather, who was sick as a result of sorcery.

Nyurdu-kurlu, nyurdu-kurlu, nyurdu-kurlu, yalumpujuku purrakuwangulpa ngarringka-jarrija. Wuraji-manulpa. Ngula-warnurnalu pardijarni nyurdukurluyijala. Yuwa, nyampunyalpa purrakulku yaarlku-yaarlku tarda-yanu. Milpa ngayingalpa yarlurnu, wanangarntarri milpangku, yuu, yuwayi. Ngulajuku jankaja kuyu, wawirri jajawangukarirla nganimpaku-palangurluyijala, nyampu manjiji kuja karlijarra nyina Molly kurrurju papardi-nyanurlayijala kuja biggest one-rla yangka kujanya yuwa. Ngula-warnuju nyurdu-kurlujuku, nyurdu-kurlujuku panu-jukujala, yakurupatuju, panu-juku manjala.

Wankaru jintalku ka nyina wankaruju, yuu, jintalku ka nyina wankaruju yalumpunya. Jintalku ka nyina Yinjirrpilki. Ngula-jangka panu-jukujala nyurdu-kurlu, nyurdu-kurlu, nyurdu-kurlu kulkurru-nyarnalu jijanunyanungu manjilki-wurru. Ngularnalu kulkurru manjijiki yapunta-jarrija, wanangarntarriji, yuu. Wanangarntarriji, nyanunguju yuwa yaliji. Ngulajuku, yuwa, yalijiki wardiji-paturlalku yilpa kuyu nyanunguju jankaja jirrama yakuru-patu-kurlangujuku. Jankajapala wawirrijarra nyanunguju. Ngula-jangka wuraji-wuraji-nyarnalu karlarrarla yapunta-jarrija kujangurlakula. Kujangurla-kularnalu yapunta-jarrija manjilki.

Kurlardalkujuku, kurlardalkujuku juka-juka-yirrarninjaku yapuntamiparlujuku-uu, nyampurlu yakurupatulu-uu yaliwiyijuku wurra.

Wartardi-purujuku-lparnalu wardu-wardu-wantija, wardu-wardu-wantija wanangarntarri. Ngula-jangka kankarlarni-parnta manjilkinkili pardijarra kajikapala-nyanu yalumpuju jurdalja-jarrajuku maju-maju-jarra malirdi-nyanuju ngajuku-palanguju, yuwayi, warlaljajuku.

There was no water at this camp. Afternoon came upon us. Then, suddenly, clouds began to gather up, and then it started raining. Just showers, not a lot of rain. So at that point we set off again with the sick man.

As we were walking, it stopped raining. We decided to stop and rest again, and so we did. As we rested, my brothers killed two kangaroos and cooked them. My grandfather was Molly Napangardi's and Japangardi's father.[1] As the sun set, my grandfather died. In the middle of nowhere we became what we call *yapunta* [orphans]. Only one of our grandfathers is still alive, and that's Yinjirrpi — the older brother of the one who died. And there in the mulga trees the kangaroos were still cooking, the kangaroos that belonged to the two brothers.

Immediately after my grandfather died my relatives began wounding themselves. They performed sorry business and prostrated themselves on the body of the deceased.

---

[1] Rosie is using 'sideways' talk here, a complex way of referring to people in Warlpiri without mentioning their names.

Warlaljajuku nyampuju.

Rdaaly-rdaaly-pakarninjaku, rdaaly-rdaaly-pakarninjaku, rdaaly-rdaaly-pakarninjaku warlamarralku, rdaaly-rdaaly-pakarninjaku, warlaljarlu-juku yalumpunyanypa … jijangkapirdinypa warrkarnu kankalarraju karntriririkirraju kalakapalanyanu malirlangurlujuku kankalarra yirrarnirra, yinyi … Ngayilki yangka warlamarralku muku-pakarninja-warnu, muku-pakarninja-warnulku kankalarra. Ngulajuku jurdaljajarrala, jurdaljala warlalja ngayilkijala-pala-nyanu jalangu-jalanguju marilkijala nganta pardimirra, jurdalja-jurdaljaju. Yuwa, manu milyiki-ngarduyulkujala kala pirntirrijalalpa karntirririjalalpa ngurrju-manu nyurru-warnu-patuju olden time-ji, karntirirrijiki jinta yuwalijiki kankalarra. Yalirlajuku kala nyanunguwiyi ngunaja yaliwarnuju. Kala jitija. 'Kari kuja ngurrjungarrarna wankaru waja ngula-warnuju waja, ngurrju waja.' Kirrirdirra-jarrija yaku-kurla-jarrinjarla, kirridirra-jarrija.

Ngula-warnurnalu wuraji-wuraji manji yampinyi-parnta, manjilkirnalu pardijarni kujarniji Jarrajarra-kurra-pinanguju karnalu kulpanjini tarnngajuku nyampu-kurraju. Ngarni-wantijarnalu yampinyiki wurajilki. Larlpunju-kurralku nganimpa-nyangukurraju Jurlarda-kurlangu-kurra, Kurru-kurlangu-kurra, Jurlarda-kurlangu-kurra pardijarnalu. Mulju-kari-kirralkurnalu pardijarra kurlarra-purda tarnngalkujuku. Yalirla manjikirla mayirnalu pirri-pungu kurlirra-purda. Pirri-pungurnalu yalirlalkujuku. Yali-warnuju ngarra kurlarrayijalarnalu karlarra pardijarra yalumpulkujuku, yalumpulkujuku, yalumpulkujuku yirnalu nyinaja yuu. Marrupunjukurrajukulpa tarda-yanu. Tarda-yanulpa yatijarra ngarlkirdipardukurra. Ngayilpa pakajaarn-yirrarnu ngarlkirdiji, pakajaarn-yirrarnulpa ngayilkijiki ngunjungkaju yarlangkaju nyiyapiyarla

Later my older brothers began to build what we call a *kantirirri* [mortuary platform] to lay my grandfather on. After they finished building it, one of my brothers climbed up the tree to the platform to test whether it was strong enough to lay my grandfather on. It was strong enough, so they raised him up and laid him on it.

Drinking water from rockholes in country to the east of Wirliyajarrayi, 1981.

In the late afternoon they made a *yampinyi* [bundle of the deceased's belongings] and grieving, they left for another place.

We went back to our country forever, to Jarrajarra, to the homeland of Larlpunju, to Jurlarda-kurlangu and to Kurrukurlangu. We headed south, travelling for a very long time from one soakage to another. On that journey we spread out. We set off to the west towards Marrupunju. Then we came to rest in the north at Ngarlkirdi-pardu. While there we collected witchetty grubs and yams.

yakajirrirla-parduju yuwali-kirra maninjarla ngulaju, yuwayi.

Yalumpu-wardingkijiki yilparnalu nyinaja yapaju manu kulpanja-yanulparnalu yangka jurrkukurra nyampukurra, jurrkukurrajuku yangka-kurrajuku jintakurra. Yangka-kurrajukulpa kulpa-kulpanja-yanurnu kalarnalu, tarnngapiya yanurnu-uu. Kalarnalu warru kulpanja-yanurnu yangka-kurrajuku jinta-kurra yalumpu-kurra.

Tarnnga-piya kalarnalu karlarrapurdalku warru pardijarra ngarra mulju-muljuwanalku, yalumpu nganimpa-nyangu-wanayijala-aa. Ngulangkarnalu pinarni jurduly-wantija yangka-kurrajuku. Miyingkalku kalarnalu yakirirlalku pangirninjarla wartardirra-jarrija.

Ngula-jangka kalarnalu pina kulpanja-yanu yangka-kurrajuku. Manu kakarrara-purdalku, kurlirra-purdalku pardija. Ngulaja kulanganta wurnturuku-ngarnti nguru-kariki-ngarnti, lawa, yangkaku-ngarntiki jintaku-ngarnti. Kalarnalu yaninja-yanu pina yangkaku-ngarntijiki. Junga. Ngulajuku. ❐

We travelled west through our country, going from soakage to soakage. Then we returned to the same place, Ngarlkirdi-pardu, and stayed there for a long time. We gathered much vegetable food there when the summer rain came. We circled to the east then, and came back. We moved around all the time, in all directions, always returning to our country. It was there that we stayed forever. ❐

Georgina Napangardi displays her painting of her country Purturlu (Mt Theo), while her son, Jangala, looks on.

22

Marrying the proper way

In the following two stories, Molly Nungarrayi and Nungarrayi describe the traditional way of becoming married. They lament the behaviour of some of today's youth, who ignore Warlpiri Law and marry whomever they choose.

According to Warlpiri Law, only an initiated man can become married, and his future, or 'promised', wife is chosen during his initiation. A man and woman can become promised to each other in two ways. In the first way, a man can become promised to the daughter of the woman who danced and held a firestick while he was being initiated. Only women whose skin name means that they can be the mother-in-law of the boy dance in this role, and, as a result, the boy's future wife is of the correct skin category. In the second way, a woman can become promised to the man who looked after her brother during his initiation.

Sometimes the promised wife is older than the promised husband, but it also happens that the promised wife is a young girl or is not yet born. The promised husband then has to wait until a daughter is born and comes of age. From the moment that he is promised, the son-in-law is obliged to supply his in-laws with gifts of meat and bush food. Later, he receives food from his mother-in-law in return for having taken care of her son during his initiation. Because the son-in-law and mother-in-law have an avoidance relationship, it is the daughter who must convey gifts of food from one to the other.

Molly Nungarrayi

WARLPIRI

Yuwayi kamparru kalarla yanu ngula-warnu jurdaljaju. Kamina kalarla palka-manu, wayi wirntija kalarla kaminaku-ngarntiji yangka yinjakulku. Kalarla ngiji mardarnu warlu.

Jampardiyi-jarrija kalarla ngulapuruju, yangka ngarrka yali mardukujaku-ngarnti witaku-ngarnti kaminaku-ngarntiwiyi. Witingkalku kalarla jampardiyi-jarrija wati. Mardukujarlu kalarla mardarnu yinjakulku. Ngula-warnu kala wapaja ngula-kurrajuku. Kala yurnungkarra-jarrinja-yanu miyalulku, kala wapanjarra-yanu-uu. Kalarla nyanunguku yirrarnu warlupuka ngayi. Kalarla yirrarnu jurdaljarlangurlu ngayi nyurruwiyi. Ngarri kalapala yirrarnu, yungu. Law-ngkapirdinypawiyi kalapala jurdaljarlangu nyinaja. Nganimpa-nyangu kujapala malirlangurlu wapaja, wapaja, jurdalja ngulanya.

Kala jalanguju lawalku. Jintangkalulku kapala ngarni walypali-piyarlulku, one

STANDARD ENGLISH

Yes, before a man married a woman or wanted a promised wife, he first had to participate in ceremonial business and perform special sacred dances. At the same time as the man danced in the ceremony, a woman — the man's future mother-in-law — danced women's sacred dances. She danced according to the Law, holding a burning firestick.

When the man's mother-in-law gave birth to a daughter, or if she already had a daughter, that little girl became the promised wife of the man. This was the way, whether she liked it or not. The girl was not allowed to marry anyone else. That was our strong Law in the old days. Our family used to travel around living according to the Law.

Not now, however. They live together in one house, sharing food like whitefellas. In mob-rlulku, ngayi. Kala jurdalja ngulalparnalu nyurruwiyi-nyurruwiyi nyinaja. 'Ngarri-jarriya kuja jungarni! Ngaju karna wawirriki yani, nyuntu ngarri-jarriya waja kuja panmarnparla, kirdapurijirla ngarri-jarriya!' Wurnalku kalalu yangka yarnkajarra. Kala panturnurra, ngapa-kari-kirrarlu kala wawirri panturnurra yangka yali jurdaljaku-ngarnti. Jungajuku kala yali miyiparduku-ngarntirli wunju kalarla karlaja-aa, yarla kala karlaja, jurdaljaku-ngarntiji-yii, karnta yali-parntarluju. 'Karinganta yalumpukula lunja-lunja-rdipijarni waja kuyu-parntaju! 'Kii, ngarri-jarriya purra-kurlangu, ngarri-jarriya waja kalya-kalya-kurra waja!' Jungajuku kalarla mardungku witangku yangka kangu, kirrminti-kangu jurdaljakuju. Kalarla kirda-nyanurlu jirrnganja-manurra. Ngula-jangka kalarla yali kuyu yangka ngulayijala kangurnu.

Kala-pala yirdi kirdarla-ngurlu yalikiji yangka jurdalja-nyanuku, kalinyanuku, kapu kalarla kuyuju wali yirrarnu mardukuja nyanungu-nyanguku yangka yali jurdaljaku. Kalarla jampardiyi-warnuku yangka yungurnu yali kuyu. Kala-pala nyinaja-aa kuyu-kurra. Kalarla kaji jaala parnkaja jurdaljaku, kalarla jarala kaji panturnu wawirripuka, yankirri jarala kaji panturnu kalarla jurdaljakuju.

Yuwa, jintamalku kalarla mardukuja yangka yali-kirra yarda yungu jintaku yalikijiki ngarrkaku. Jurdalja warlarlaljaku kalarla yarda yungu ngawurru-nyanupuka. Yuwa, ngawurrunyanulku kalarla yarda yungu. Jirrama-kari kala-palangu mardarnu yangka kamparru-warnujarra, yangka kapirdi-nyanujarra jintangkujuku. Ngulajangkalurla jinta-karilki yangka yarda yungu yali jintakujuku.

Warntamarrirla kala nyinaja junga nyurruwiyi, nyurruwiyi. Kalarla nguurl-kangu ngaka yali kukurnu-nyanukuju milarninjarla. Junga kala warntamarri-manu.

the olden time the in-laws used to live separately. A husband would tell his wife, 'Go straight to your mother. I'm going for kangaroo. You go to your mother and father and stay there while I'm away.' The man then left. He speared a kangaroo and then went to another waterhole. A man would kill kangaroo to share with his father-in-law. Yes, he'd dig bush yams for his mother-in-law. 'That man is coming with food and kangaroo,' a mother would say to her daughter. 'Take some water to your husband now.' Truly, she took water in her little water carrier and carried it on her hip to her father-in-law. Her father helped her to carry the water, and then he'd bring the fresh meat back to his wife.

Fathers and sons would save meat for their in-laws and their wives. They'd hunt kangaroos and emus for their in-laws.

Yes, they would give another wife to that man in the same way that they had given him wives before. That is, to their own son-in-law they then gave the younger sister of his wives. He already had two wives, and then they gave the wife's younger sister as a third wife to the same man. In the olden time a man would sleep among many wives. At the same time he would choose one of his wives for his younger brother. Yes, this is how they lived. One man lived with many wives, with many women. Yes, they sometimes used to have as many as seven wives in the

Ngarrka jintangku kala warntamarri-manu. Mardukuja panu warntamarri-manu kala. Yuwayi, wirlki-puka, wirlki kalalu mardarnu nyurruwiyi, nyurruwiyi, yuwayi.

Yuwayi kala kurdijiki-ngarntiji, kirri-kari-jangka kala mulju-ngurlu, mulju-ngurlu kujarni kulpanja-yanurnu. Kala ngulangurlu kulpanja-yanurnu kujarni. Kurlarni kala kulpajarni yulpayiwana-wana. Kala yaninja-yanurnu kurlarni-kurlarni kujarni. Kala manu jakurdu-kurdu. Kala kurdu yali parnkaja. Yangka yali marna-kurra-warnu-jangkarlangu wirntinja-warnurlangu kala manu, kala manu. Kala turnu-jarrinja-yanurnu ngarrkangkarla. Kala pardija jakurdu-kurdu jilkajaku-ngarduyulku-jala. ❐

old days.

Yes, the people came from different soakages and gathered together in one place for ceremonies. They used to come from the south and follow the creek. They came from the south. They'd send an initiate out to gather up more people, and he'd bring them back to that same ceremonial place where he'd come from. A number would always come to that place and then wait for the others to arrive. They always gathered together like this for ceremonies. ❐

Yarla *(bush yams). A mother-in-law gives food such as yams to her son-in-law for having looked after her son in men's business during 'young man time'.*

Molly Nungarrayi

Now, women and men marry any time they like at any age. We still perform the ceremonial dances for promising a wife to a man, but they don't keep the promises now. Although a woman should give her daughter to the promised husband, she doesn't take it seriously now. She lets her daughter run off with any man she likes. It also happens that a man has a promised wife, but he doesn't take it seriously either. He would rather run off with any woman he likes. They think sacred dancing is a game, and they just perform it for nothing. Truly.

When the man and his mother-in-law are true and honest to each other, the promised wife is given to her husband, and the man accepts her as he should. When the time arrives and the girl is old enough to be given, then the man and his mother-in-law are not allowed to look at each other or go near each other. This is because they became 'in-laws' when they both performed the sacred dances.

Another way for a man to get a wife is when the man was only a boy and had to be caught in order to become initiated. The men, who were generally his brothers, would grab the boy and take him to his brother-in-law (whom we call *juka* or *panji*), who would care for him out bush. Before the start of the ceremony, the boy would be taken by his brother-in-law and shown the soakages and places on the land. This was in our time, a long time ago. He [the brother-in-law] would gather up all the boy's relatives in preparation for the initiation ceremony. He would gather them up and bring them back to the place where the ceremony was to be held.

When all the relatives had arrived, the ceremony would begin. Men and women would participate in the sacred dances. Each skin group followed their father's Jukurrpa. Each boy would perform his father's Jukurrpa dance. This would continue for a week or two, while the boy stayed in the bush. He was not allowed to come into the camp and be seen by his mother and relatives.

When the ceremonies had finished the boy, who was now a man and attired in lengths of material, would be brought out of the bush by his brother-in-law to his mothers and aunties. They would be waiting to release him [from the ceremonial business] so that he was free to walk around the camp. After that was done he was finished, he was now an initiated man. He would still have to camp with his brother-in-law for a night or two after his release.

And what would the brother-in-law receive in return for looking after the boy in the bush and making him a man? His sister. He would receive the boy's sister as his promised wife. The boy's mother had to accept this, because the brother-in-law had looked after her son out bush. In doing so, the boy's brother-in-law had become the mother's 'in-law', and they were not allowed to go near each other now. However, the mother-in-law had to look after her son-in-law in return for his having looked after her son in the business camp out bush. She had to send him food all the time. She gave food — such as yams or goannas that she collected while out hunting — to her daughter to take to her husband, because as his mother-in-law she was not allowed to take the food to him herself.

It would also work the other way. The man had to look after his mother-in-law by providing her with food. Whatever bush food he brought back from hunting he gave to his mother-in-law. He would ask his promised wife to take the food to her mother — the person who had given him his wife. In this way there were no arguments over food. They would both look after each other in return for having done something for each other. That was how it was a long time ago. The end. ❒

Nungarrayi

The mother-in-law and son-in-law used to look after each other until the little girl grew older. This was the olden time Law for the in-laws. The son-in-law looked after his promised wife's mother. The mother let her daughter grow up for the husband who was promised during initiation ceremonies. That girl couldn't go to any man except the promised husband, otherwise they'd all have a big fight. When the promised man and woman married and they had a child together, then the girl's parents became the grand-mother and grandfather of that child, who belonged to the promised husband, not to any other man. The mother and father of the girl used to look after her for the promised husband — not for anyone else.

The son-in-law used to bring home meat for his mother-in-law. She told her daughter to take seed cakes, yams and *wanakiji* fruit to him. The son-in-law gave kangaroo and emu meat to his wife to take to her mother. Nowadays some people act like white people and don't look after their relatives properly.

The husband would go camping out and tell his wife to stay with her parents. The girl's mother dug for yams and shared them with her son-in-law when he brought back meat for them. The mother used to tell her daughter to give water to her husband. He used to share meat with his father-in-law. Maybe the father would give another young wife to him because he was a good son-in-law. In the olden time a generous young man would be rich, having seven or eight wives. That was in the olden time when they had proper Law. ❐

May Napurrula and children hunting for **jurlarda** *(bush honey), 1977.*

A jealous fight

Despite the fact that Warlpiri Law specifies the correct marriage partners for men and women, 'wrong way' love affairs with others were (and remain) common. Here Nungarrayi describes how people dealt with such affairs in the old days.

Nungarrayi

In the old days, when men used to have jealous fights, the only weapons they used were spears and stone knives. The men used to spear each other in the thigh, or cut each other with stone knives.

For example, there was a girlfriend and boyfriend who ran off to the bush to meet each other without anyone knowing. The woman was the promised wife of an old man. As the sun went down and it grew dark, people suddenly realised that the woman and man had run off as lovers. They let the old man know by telling him, 'A man ran off with your wife. You'd better give him a good hiding or spear him in the leg.'

After a few days in the bush the lovers returned to be speared by the old man. The man and woman came out into an open place, and the young man, without a shield or anything to protect himself and with only emu feathers hanging from his sides, started high stepping.[1] The woman carried a fighting stick and stood in front of her lover, facing her promised husband. Then the woman said to her lover's mother, her promised husband and her own relatives, 'Come on, attack us now. We are here, ready.' Then the old man got his spears ready while the other people said to him, 'Go on, spear him properly. Give him a lesson.' The woman placed herself between the two men, and the old man dragged her to his side, saying, 'Come here by my side. I'm your husband.' Then the old man threw a spear at the young man.

Little Napurrula, Nungarrayi and Nampijinpa mimic ritualised steps performed by women as a prelude to fighting.

The young man sat down facing away, with his back to the old man. Quickly the old man got out his stone knife and cut the young man on the back of his shoulders. Then relatives of the two men announced, 'No-one else is going to join in the fight. The fight is between these two only.'

So the woman went home with the old man, and the old man said to the young man, 'Go now.' The old man was the brother of the young man. The young man's mother, father, aunts and uncles told him, as they helped him up, 'You'd better not touch his wife again. Why can't you stick with your own promised wife? Go home with her. Don't ever run off like that again with the old man's wife. Why did you do this to your brother?' ❑

---

[1] As a prelude to ritualised conflict, men perform high stepping movements that signal their readiness to face attacks by boomerang or spear.

Singing her man

Here Nangala recounts how a woman successfully attracted and married her chosen man by singing love songs to him.

Milly Nangala

WARLPIRI	STANDARD ENGLISH

Mungalyurrulpalu turnu-jarrinjanurnu purlapaku-ngarnti. Manu panu-wapaja mungalyurru-warnu miyiki manu kuyuku-purda. Mirntangali-warnujulu pina yanurnu kuyu-kurlu manu miyi-kirli. Manu murnma-jukulpa kuyuju jankaja, manu miyi yarla. Ngula-warnuju wilypi-maninjarlalpalu jarnngi-jarnngi manu kuyu wawirriji manu yarlalpalu wilypi-maninjarla payi-kirra yirrarnu yangka walyka-jarrinjaku ngarnti. Manulpalu ngarnu.

Some people gathered together in the morning for a *purlapa* [corroboree]. Others went hunting and returned in the mid morning with food. They started cooking kangaroo and bush potatoes and then, when it was cooked, they took the food out of the fire and let it cool down a bit. The food was shared around and then people ate it.

Pirda-parnta pirda-parntalkulpalu turnu-jarrinjanurnu yangka yama-kurra purlapaku-ngarnti. Kala karnta jintangkulpa yunjumu-karirli yunparnu ngarrka yalikilparla waninja nyinanja kujalpa majardi-kurlurlu pajurnu kurlarda-kurlurlu, manu jakarla-kurlurlupa yunparnu.

After they'd finished eating they gathered together in the shade. One woman sat facing away from the others. She was singing and she was falling in love with the man who wore the pubic tassel and a pearl shell necklace and had a spear.

Mungalyurru-karirlalkulpalu yangka yakarra-pardijarla marna warru pajurnu yangka wirlinyiki-ngarntirli. Junga-jukulu yanu wirlinyiji, manu panu-karijilpalu marna warru pajurnu yangka mardukuruku ngurrju-maninjaku pularpaku-ngarnti yungulu pinyi.

The following morning the men looked around for vegetable down, and then some people went out hunting. Others stayed back looking for more vegetable down, getting ready for the purlapa.

Manulpalu karnta-karntaju turnu-jarrinjanurnu yali-kirra ngarrka patu-kurra kujalpalu kamparru-warnu nyinaja yunparninjarla. Manulpalu-jana purrpu pakarnu karntarluju. Kala karnta jintangkulparla waninjarlu yunparnu ngarrka yaliki, kujalparla yunparnu majardi-kirli kurlarda-kurlu manu jakarla-kurlurlu Majunparla.

While the men began singing, the women gathered together and started singing to the men. The women were clapping their hands in their laps to the beat. One of the women sang a different song, a love song, to one of the men, who was looking attractive in his ceremonial attire and singing with the men. This happened at Majunpa.

Ngula-warnuju karnta yalirlijilparla warrarda yunparnu ngarrka yaliki-juku, manu karnta-karijilparla kuja-puta

The woman continued to sing to the man, and the other women heard her and told her, 'Sing properly, they might hear

wangkaja, 'Yuwa jungarnirli yunpaka kaji kangkulu yapangku purdanyani.' Lawa-jukurla puta wangkaja karnta-kuju warra-rdalparla yunparnu ngarrka yaliki-juku. Karnta yalijilpa-nyanu kuja wangkaja, 'Yuwa ngamardi-nyanurlangu yilpa kurnta-ngarrikarla yapa-karirli-piya kuja kalu yangka jungarnirli yunparni.'

Mirntangali-warnujulu yapa yangka patujulu pina-yanurnu kuyu wawirri-kirli manu miyi yarla-kurlu. Ngula-warnuju, kuyu manu miyiljilpa nyurru-jankaja warlungkalku. Kuyu wawirri manu miyi yarlalpalu wilypimanu murntulku, manulpalu jarnngi-jarnngi maninjarla ngarnu, manulu-jana yapaku muku yungu.

Wuraji-wurajilpalu turnu-jarrijanurnu yangka purlapaku-ngarnti, manu karnta-karntalpalu-jana purrpu-pakarnu kujalpalu yunparnu wati-paturlu manu karnta-karntarlu. Kala karnta jintangkulparla ngarrka yaliki-juku warrarda yunparnu, waninja-nyinajalparla kujalpa majardi-kirli pajarnu manu kurlarda-kurlurlu manu jakarla-kurlurlu majarnu yunparninja-kurrarlu.

Ngulalu purlapa-jangka pina-pina yanu ngurra-kurralku, yungulu-jana marrirdilki karnta yangkaku manu ngarrka nyanungu ngulalpa purlapa yunparnu karntangku, ngarrurnulu-jana nyinaya pala tarnngalku. ❐

you.' But the woman didn't take any notice of the others — she just kept on singing. The women said to each other, 'Her mother should tell her to sing like everyone else.'

In the mid morning, the others came back from hunting with more kangaroos and bush potatoes, which they cooked in the fire. After the food was cooked they cut it in pieces and shared it around with others in the camp, and then everyone ate it.

Later in the afternoon everyone gathered for the purlapa. The women began singing for the men, and that same woman continued to sing for the man who looked so good singing in his ceremonial attire.

After the purlapa had finished, the women's relations decided to let her marry the man, and told them to stay together forever. ❐

Snake dreaming by Carole Napaljarri Kitson. Linocut print, 1993

Part Two

Olden time: the first white men

Passing through: Harry Henty

In the following oral history, Milly Nangala tells of one of the earliest remembered encounters with a white man on the Lander River. The event occurred when Harry Henty drove cattle through the area in the early 1920s.[1] Shortly after this episode he returned to the area and built a bush cattle yard a few kilometres south of Mount Barkly, at a place called Pirraparnta-kurlangu. His stay in Lander country was brief, however. Henty left to take up a grazing licence at Frew River Station in the east, where he was killed in 1929 by an Aboriginal man called Willaberta Jack, who was acting in self-defence.[2] Warlpiri recall other white men who travelled down the Lander on their way to the Granites goldfields (to the north-west of Willowra).[3] One of these was Joe Brown, a contractor who carted goods on camels and horses. In 1921, with Jimmy Jungarrayi, an Aboriginal man from Gordon Downs who acted as his horsetailer, Brown 'discovered' Yinapaka, a lake at the floodout of the Lander, which was renamed Lake Surprise.[4]

Milly Nangala

At Patirlirri they saw three whitefellas coming with four Aboriginal people. The Japaljarris were performing the Tarntarnngali ceremony. The whitefellas came with camels and mules. Aborigines had no clothes. Someone came closer with a horse and saw that they were naked. Only pubic coverings. They were doing the ceremony for Jurrpunju. The whitefellas gathered people together and put food down. Harry Henty gave them trousers and shirts. He brought them flour and told the people to taste it. They tasted it, it was good. He gave them flour, tea, soap, tobacco and jam. All the children were playing, and their mothers called out, 'Come and taste this flour and tea, it's good.' After Harry Henty gave them clothes, he went away. He followed the creek, looking for other people. He told people that he'd come back. ❒

---

[1] At the time, Henty held a grazing licence over Yanmajirri country near Ti Tree.
[2] See Peter Horsetailer's account of this incident in Koch, 1993:41–46.
[3] See Alec Jupurrula Wilson's account of first contact between whites and Warlpiri to the north-west of Willowra in Read and Read, 1991:3–4.
[4] Hartwig, 1960:12.

A whitefella comes to stay: Nugget Morton

William J. Morton — or 'Nugget' as he was known — first passed through the Lander River area en route to the Tanami goldfields in the early 1920s. In 1923, for the sum of twenty-nine pounds, he took out a grazing licence (GL 357) for four hundred square miles on Lander Warlpiri country. Licensed to stock one beast per square mile, Morton drove cattle to Willowra from Victoria River Downs. He took on B. S. Sandford as a partner in 1924, and they named their holding 'Broadmeadows', in reference to the broad spinifex plains which surround the Lander River. Morton and Sandford then took out a second grazing licence (GL 366) for two hundred and fifty square miles, immediately to the west of the first. They cancelled the northernmost 150 square miles of the first grazing licence upon finding out that the river 'runs north-west and the said 150 square miles is useless to us being all spinifex.' [1] *Morton and Sandford replaced the lost block with another grazing licence (GL 478) lower down the Lander, to the north of GL 366.*

In 1927 G. J. Murray took out a grazing licence (GL 693) along Morton and Sandford's southern boundary near Pawu, or Mount Barkly, as it is called in English.[2] *In the same year J. Wickham and J. Matthews stocked the area to the east of Willowra, known today as Old Mount Peake.*

These newcomers were lawless, taking no account of Aboriginal Law and little of European. For years they had lived recklessly on the outback frontier, and, as European settlement intensified, they followed the shrinking stretches of Aboriginal-occupied land.[3] *It seems that part of the attraction of the Warlpiri lands for these whites lay in its isolation from European centres. Unlike the neighbouring Yanmajirri territory, Lander Warlpiri country was far enough from the Overland Telegraph Line not to have been 'settled' by whites until well into the twentieth century.*

In response to the onslaught of these seasoned 'pioneers', Lander Warlpiri fought back in what amounted to a guerilla-style resistance. At first they picked off bullocks, spearing them for meat. Milly Nangala's story recounts how **kurdaitcha** *men killed cattle for meat.*

Milly Nangala

In the olden days Nugget Morton, a whitefella, came to Mud Hut. He was walking around Wirliyajarrayi. We were frightened, so we stayed in the bush near Partirlirri. We used to sneak around and get water at night from the Mud Hut soakage. After it rained we went further out to other rockholes and soakages. We stayed at soakages west of Kajuru, and then we went to Patirlirri. We walked around that area, around and around. From Patirlirri we went to Liirlpari, then to Pawu, Yinjirrpi-kirlangu and Ngarnka [Mount Leichhardt]. We stayed in the bush because we were frightened. Whitefellas walked around with camels and horses near the hills at Pawu and Ngarnka. They were looking for Aboriginal people. We

---

[1] Australian Archives (NT): F28; GL 478.

[2] Australian Archives (NT): F28; GL 481.

[3] Jimmy Wickham, for example, spent many years in the Kimberley before coming to the Territory. He was sentenced to five years in jail with hard labour after being caught on the Frew River duffing cattle from Lake Nash Station (Kimber, 1986:106; see also Cole, 1988:26–27). According to the Aboriginal storyteller Alfie Deakin, Wickham was a crook, and lived for a period of time between Limbunya and Mistake Creek (Shaw, 1992:125).

hid in the hills. Our family used to take us away from that angry whiteman. We'd climb down the hills and get water when he'd gone away.

When Nugget Morton brought cattle, this was the first time that I'd tasted [bullock] meat. The *kurdaitcha* man would steal it. All the kurdaitcha men used to kill the bullocks, and we became used to eating bullock meat. Some people were living at Larlpunju when Wickham came to Willowra. Morton used to stay at Mud Hut. Another whiteman, called Tilmouth, came to Mud Hut. He gave people some food. Tilmouth gave flour, tea, jam and tobacco to my grandmother. All the whitefellas were taking Aboriginal women, and the men were getting jealous. ❐

Dinner camp: Topsy Nangala cooks **wardapi** *(Sand Monitor) while Lady Nampijinpa (centre) and May Napurrula (right) look on.*

Conflict at Yurrkuru (Brookes Soak): a whitefella stole my grandmother

The first whites on the Lander were single men who struck up relationships with Aboriginal women. At times they used overt force. The stockman Walter Smith has described, for example, how Nugget Morton captured an albino woman, 'but when she resisted his over-tures, had shot her.' [1] While, undoubtedly, relationships developed that would not have involved direct force, the taking of an Aboriginal 'girlfriend' by a European was never a simple matter, because all Lander Warlpiri women were either married or promised to an Aboriginal man. On occasions, Aboriginal men collaborated with whites in the temporary exchange of women for food and tobacco. Conflict broke out, however, when the whites refused to return the women to their husbands. Such an incident occurred on 7 August 1928, when the European Fred Brookes was killed by an Aboriginal man on the headwaters of the Lander River near Coniston, seventy-two miles south of Willowra. Rosie Nungarrayi speaks of that event here.[2] The death of Brookes resulted in the wanton murder of innocent Aborigines in the Coniston area, as a police party led by Constable Murray 'investigated' the incident.[3]

Rosie Nungarrayi

At Yurrkuru, my grandfather killed a whitefella. He hit the whitefella because the whitefella stole his wife. That old lady was my grandmother, a Napurrula. She was frightened when that whitefella took her — that's why the old man hit him. After that the old man ran up to the hills to hide. My grandfather was living in the hills, in a cave. That's what saved his life while the police were out looking for him. He stayed in the hills. They didn't find him, because he was sitting in the cave. ❐

---

[1] Kimber, 1986:108–109. Accounts of violence between whites and blacks over Aboriginal women are widespread. See, for example, the accounts in Koch, 1993:39–46.

[2] Another version of the incident is recounted by Blind Alec Jupurrula and Engineer Jack Japaljarri in Read and Read, 1991:35–37.

[3] See Read and Read, 1991, for additional information on the killings in the Coniston area.

Trouble at Boomerang Hole

In addition to cattle killing and trouble over women, a severe drought on the Lander River fuelled the hostility between Aborigines and the white settlers as they competed for control of the waterholes. Morton had set up camps at Mud Hut (Yardingurnangu), Eight Mile (Minapungu), and Boomerang (Jangan-kurlangu) waterholes. Tilmouth was at Whitestone (Liirlpari), and Wickham occupied Willowra (Wirliyajarrayi) waterholes. Their cattle polluted and depleted the precious waterholes that supported the Aborigines along the Lander River. By late 1928, only Jangan-kurlangu had water, and Morton was in occupation. On 28 August, Morton was attacked by three Warlpiri at the waterhole.[1] In the following account, Kitty Napangardi tells G. Napangardi (GN) and P. Vaarzon-Morel (PVM) about the events at Boomerang Waterhole, as they were told to her by another woman.

Kitty tells the story in Aboriginal English. A standard English translation follows.

Kitty Napangardi

ABORIGINAL ENGLISH	STANDARD ENGLISH
KN: Story I bin — nother lady bin tellembout longa mefella Nugget Morton. Well him bin walking round longa Nungarrayi mob. Well him bin young girl — no Lucy first. Well him — that whitefella — bin tellem, 'Youfella killem killer?'	KN: Another lady told me the story about Nugget Morton. He'd been walking around Nungarryi and some others — this was when Nungarrayi was a young girl, before she had Lucy. Morton asked someone, 'Did you people kill a bullock?'
GN: Was Peggy born then?	*GN: Was Peggy born at that time?*
PVM: No, different time.	*PVM: No, it was a different time.*
GN: Before Peggy mayi?	*GN: Before Peggy?*
KN: No, Lucy first one. And that Molly, him bin young girl.	KN: Yes, Lucy was born first. Molly was still a young girl.
GN: And old Rosie, Lucy's mother now.	*GN: And Lucy's mother, Rosie, was still a young girl.*
KN: All right. Reckon that whitefella bin muck around longa him, and that friend longa him. His girl, him bin Emily eh? *Yapirliyipuraji.* Him bin tellem that whitefella, 'You go back, takem back what's-a-name, lettem go horses.' Him bin walking	KN: All right. They reckoned that Morton had mucked around with Nungarrayi. Nungarrayi's friend, Emily, was his girlfriend. Her grandfather told Morton, 'You leave here and take your horses with you.' Morton had been walking around

---

[1] Another version of the Nugget Morton incident is recounted by Willowra Jimmy Jungarrayi and Jampijinpa in Read and Read, 1991.

*Cutting wood which will be used to make **kuturu**, women's dancing and fighting sticks (also known as **nullah-nullahs**).*

round longa that Boomerang way [laughter]. All right. 'Youfella bin eatem *puluku*?' [Morton asked]. 'Yeah, himfella reckon can have killer, eatem.'

GN: *She bin tellem — because she bin have girlfriend with him, 'Oh, you can eat.'*

KN: Yeah, bullock, anything. All right. Mefella bin — me bin behind yet, little girl, Ti Tree way.

PVM: *That was with Nungarrayi?*

KN: Yeah, fat one. All right. Him bin there, well 'nother one mob bin tellem, 'Girl gottem kid. You gotta run away Tennant Creek, or Barrow Creek or Tennant Creek or youfella go Banka Banka.' True right. Allabout bin line up — all together that, going up. And man bin there. Well, that man bin there, Nugget Morton. That one bin bringem trouble.

Boomerang Hole. Morton asked, 'Did you fellows eat a bullock?' We replied, 'Yes. They said we could have a killer.'

GN: *She had told them that they could have a killer, because she was his girlfriend.*

KN: Yes, a bullock or something. All right. At the time I was only a little girl and living at Ti Tree.

PVM: *That was with Nungarrayi?*

KN: Yes, Nungarrayi, the fat one. All right. Some other people said that Morton had got a young girl pregnant, and that they'd have to run away north to Tennant Creek, Barrow Creek or Banka Banka. That's true. Well they all gathered together. Nugget Morton was there. He's the one that caused the trouble.

PVM: *Maju maju!*

KN: Hmmm, maju maju one. Well that *karnta* Nampijinpa, him bin sleepin' yet. And that *walypali* here. Looking after horses yet that girl. And little rifle there — revolver think [laughter], yeah revolver, I think, revolver. Well sit down — big man that Nugget Morton, not little one, fat one.

GN: *He was a big man?*

KN: Yeah. Right, allabout bin comin' up workin', I think working boy, 'Me wantem tucker, meat.' That walypali bin cuttem — give it like that. 'Na, doublem now.' Twofella bin hang on longa 'nother arm, 'nother arm, now. Finish. That old man old fella bin startem again, beltem about 'nother one again, longa 'nother tree again. Talk about walypali lettem — nulla nullas, boomerang, too big! Allabout bin pokem everything, beltem round.

GN: *Was bashing up Nugget?*

KN: Yeah.

PVM: *And who was that Nampijinpa that he was with?* Nyurnu *or* palka?

KN: Nyurnu that one. His name Emily. Allabout bin beltem-bout again, biggest hiding again allabout bin givit. No horses.

PVM: *All the* yapa *gave that Nampijinpa a hiding?*

KN: Yeah, and same this walypali too. Now that walypali bin chuckem anyway. Now 'nother mob bin hang on there. Well him bin shakem like that, and pooo [laughter] — whole lot bin fall down.

GN: *He bin shake them all off and throw them.*

PVM: *A bad man!*

KN: Yes, a bad one. Well Nampijinpa, Morton's horsetailer, was still sleeping, and the whitefella was close by. He had a rifle — no, I think it was a revolver. Well Morton sat down — he was a big fat man, not a small one.

GN: *He was a big man?*

KN: Yes. The working boys came up to Morton and said, 'We want some tucker, some meat.' Morton cut off some meat and gave it to them, but they said, 'No, we want double the amount.' Then one man grabbed Morton by an arm, and another man held his other arm. That was it. Morton fought back and belted them from tree to tree. He really let them have it. It was a really big fight, and people were hitting Morton with fighting sticks and boomerangs.

GN: *They were bashing up Nugget?*

KN: Yes.

PVM: *And who was that Nampijinpa who was with him? Is she alive or dead today?*

KN: She's dead. Her name was Emily. As there were no horses there for her to get away, they gave her a thrashing too.

PVM: *All the Aboriginal people were giving that Nampijinpa a hiding?*

KN: Yes, and they were giving the white man one too, until he shook them off, but then some others attacked him. Well, Morton shook them off again, sending them sprawling.

GN: *He shook them off and threw them down.*

KN: Yeah, yeah, and allabout bin pokem this one [pointing to her back].

PVM: *In the back yeah.*

KN: Everyway. Too big him bin doing, like that one.

PVM: *Just chucking them away?*

KN: And holdem again, 'nother two bin holdem this arm, same here, and 'nother one bin sitting down.

GN: *[Laughter] 'Nother one jumped right on his back?*

KN: *Yuwayi* … That *wankili* one, *yanurnu.* Well him bin comin' up, you know, crawl up longa that swag — rifle bin there, revolver. Well, him bin see-em there, him bin getem that rifle. Some fella bin tired now. Oh him bin gettem bang! Him bin fall down now, that man. That woman bin run.

PVM: *Nugget Morton?*

KN: Him bin fall down. All gone! That's all together. Him bin catchem up, anymore. Him bin catchem one, that's finish. That woman bin go run. Oh, crippled, every-thing — arm. Crippled. Him bin bandage-bout flour bag, you know?

PVM: *Nugget Morton bandaged it?*

KN: Yeah, him bin bandage-bout. What's-a-name bin there, Mud Hut, I think, Sandford man. Sandford, whiteman. Him bin there sittin' down. Yeah, his son again, I think. You know, friend longin' to him. Nugget Morton. Camel man.

And Nungarrayi mob bin run this way again, longa Barkly. And somefella gone that way, altogether, that one. And that

KN: Yes, and everyone was hitting him in the back.

PVM: *In his back, yes.*

KN: Wherever they could. He was so big.

PVM: *He was fending them off?*

KN: Then they'd get hold of him again, with two on one arm and someone else jumping on his back.

GN: *Someone else jumped right on his back?*

KN: Yes. My cousin — he's dead now. Well then Morton crawled over to his swag to get his rifle — his revolver. The others were tired out when Morton grabbed his rifle and fired a shot. One man fell down and a woman ran away.

PVM: *Nugget Morton?*

KN: He fell down exhausted. Everyone had gone. He'd shot one man. Emily ran away then. Morton was in a bad way. He tied his crippled arm up using a flour bag for a sling.

PVM: *Nugget Morton tied it up?*

KN: Yes, he tied it up. Sandford was camped at Mud Hut at the time. I think Sandford was a friend of Morton's, you know — like a son. Sandford used to get around on camels.

Well, Nungarrayi and some of the others ran this way, towards Mount Barkly, and others went another way. In fact, Nungarrayi ended up near Ti Tree.

Nungarrayi bin come back right here, right up Ti Tree way. All right, that Nampijinpa bin washem-bout now — waterhole-rla. Same himself swell up. Twofella bin comin' back, leavem swag. Come back longa Sandford.

All right. Him bin come back, bandage-em now. Allabout bin sendem him now, longa Ti Tree. That mob bin bandage-em-bout now. And washem-bout. Him bin dumpem there again, that Nampijinpa. Dead one. Him bin leave-em there. Gone get policeman now, Kumunjayi I think, Murray. Him bin longa Barrow Creek. Young fella, him bin callem up that one. Got horses, no car.

PVM: That Nampijinpa palka?

KN: Nothing, pass away longa Alice now. All right, young girl again. He bin go callem up Randall, I think.

PVM: Randall Stafford?

KN: Yeah. Old Randall bin longa Coniston eh?

PVM: Yeah.

KN: And 'nother one all bin killem there again eh? Two boy bin come back.

PVM: Brookes? At Brookes Soakage?

KN: Yeah. Him and 'nother, Fred, I think.

PVM: Yeah, that's right, Fred, Fred Brookes.

KN: Yeah, [laughter] that one. Nugget all bin gettem. And that one, allabout bin fin-ishem, that 'nother one. And that little boy — two — Kipper and dead fella. Twofella

All right. Well, Nampijinpa was also all swollen up [from the beating] and washed herself in Boomerang Waterhole. Then Morton set off to Sandford's place, leaving his swag behind.

All right. Well, after Sandford helped Morton wash up and helped bandage him, Morton rode to Ti Tree to get Kumunjayi — the policeman, Murray. He left Nampijinpa behind sick. At the time Murray was at Barrow Creek. He was still young then and got about on horses — there were no cars.

PVM: Is that Nampijinpa still alive?

KN: No, she passed away in Alice Springs. I think she must have been the one who called up Randall.

PVM: Randall Stafford?

KN: Yeah. Old Randall was at Coniston Station, wasn't he?

PVM: Yeah.

KN: And there'd been a big fight there too, hadn't there? Two Aboriginal men from there told us about it.

PVM: That was Brookes, at Brookes Soak?

KN: Yes that's the name of the man now, and I think his other name was Fred.

PVM: Yeah, that's right, Fred, Fred Brookes.

KN: Yeah, that one. Well, Nugget fought off his attackers, but Brookes — they finished him off. And those two boys, Kipper, and another one who is dead now — those two bin musterin' that bullock — cow again, camel. Tellem longa that old Randall, 'Whitefella is dead!' 'All right, you twofella wait, policeman comin' up.' Nugget Morton bin bringem right up there, cleanem up. Mefella bin five yet — little kid, I think. Cleanem up, oh, everyway [said in a deep voice].

PVM: Shooting people?

KN: Mmm, yeah, everyway alla-fella bin. All right, you know that Jarrajarra that way?

GN: Jarrajarra?

KN: Yeah, and Pirtipirti? That one, that's Kaytetye ah, Warumungu — somefella him bin havem there. Well 'nother one bin talk, 'Oh, this one different again.' Barrow Creek mob and Tennant Creek, Warumungu, Kaytetye. I don't know [about] Warlpiri. All right, him bin comin' up followem that 'nother creek now — Hanson way, that one. Him bin followem that way, that policeman. No bullet, anything, nothing. And one Pintupi, I think. Him bin helpem. Him bin just tellem that old Murray, 'Eh, this one never killem alla-onefella.' Him bin cleanem up and shootem like dog. Him bin die now, that policeman. Finish. Him bin have …

PVM: That Alec Wilson was with that Murray, wasn't he? Alec Wilson?

KN: Yeah, you're right. That one. Two half-caste, I think. Twofella bin get away. And Aboriginal all dead. Mustered-up, finish. Pintupi bin — that man Pintupi bin summonsem now, that policeman. Nugget Morton bin shift-along that what's-a-name now, Anningie. Him bin livin' there now.

had been mustering bullocks — well, cows and camels — and they told old Randall, 'The white man is dead.' Stafford told them, 'Right, you wait for the policeman to come.' Nugget Morton brought Murray up there, and they cleaned everyone up. I was only a little kid of five at the time, I think. Oh, they rode all around shooting people everywhere.

PVM: Shooting people?

KN: Mmmm, yeah, they went everywhere. All right. You know Jarrajarra, in that direction?

GN: Jarrajarra?

KN: Yeah, and Pirtipirti? That place. They're in Kaytetye country, aren't they? Oh, there were some Warumungu there at the time also. Someone said that there were a lot of different people there: people from Barrow Creek and Tennant Creek; Warumungu and Kaytetye. But I don't know if there were any Warlpiri. All right. The policeman Murray tracked people all the way up the Hanson Creek. I think it was a Pintupi man who helped him. He helped him because he thought Murray had no bullets, nothing. He said, 'Oh he'll never shoot anyone.' But Murray cleaned the people up. He shot them just like they were dogs. Well Murray is dead now.

PVM: That Alec Wilson was with Murray wasn't he?

KN: Yeah, you're right. That's him. I think there were two half-castes. Two of them got away. And the Aborigines were all shot. Mustered up. Dead. That Pintupi man summoned the policeman. Nugget Morton then shifted away from the area and went to live at Anningie.

Shiftem away. Wickham bin shift here now, this way. Walk around quiet place here now. Wild dog bin here, this country. And pussycat, kangaroo, rabbit, anything, possum, that's all. Mud Hut-rla. Right, allabout bin go back again, shiftem you know. All right, 'You got to gettem that Willowra.' All right. Him bin livin' longa Mud Hut, not here. This one mefella bin use-em this one, and that what's-a-name well there. ❐

Then Wickham came to live here at Willowra. It was a quiet place then. I'd walk around, and there'd be only wild dogs here; and some cats, kangaroos, rabbits and possums — that's all. Well, then Wickham and the other white men shifted out to Mud Hut and told others to look after Willowra. We took care of things at Willowra and that well — what's its name again? ❐

A shooting at Liirlpari (Whitestone)

Soon after the incident at Jangan-kurlangu (Boomerang Waterhole), Tilmouth was attacked at Liirlpari. According to Rosie Nungarrayi, he retaliated by shooting an old Jungarrayi who worked for him.

Rosie Nungarrayi

An old Jungarrayi was living there at Liirlpari at the time, uncle for old Ruby Nampijinpa and Alfie Jampijinpa. He was working for a whitefella there called Tilmouth. That old Jungarrayi was working for him, but Tilmouth shot him dead with a rifle. ❐

The ruins of old Anningie homestead on the road to Wirliyajarrayi.

The massacres

Following a request by Morton to arrest his attackers, Constable Murray set out for Willowra with Morton, a small Aboriginal boy named Wilson, and fourteen horses. They rode down the Lander and Hanson rivers seeking out Aboriginal encampments. Equipped only with spears, fighting sticks and boomerangs, Warlpiri were no match for the gun-brandishing intruders, and it is said that over a hundred innocent people were slaughtered.

Because of the reports of the killings in overseas newspapers and agitation by church missionary societies, in 1929 an official board of inquiry was set up to investigate the actions of the punitive party. Statements were taken from Morton, Tilmouth, a missionary based at Ti Tree called Miss Annie Locke, and Police Constable Murray. According to Murray and Morton, the punitive party shot four Warlpiri at Tomahawk Waterhole, then rode past Boomerang Waterhole (Jangan-kurlangu) and on to Circle Well, where they shot two more men. They then rode to Wajinpulungku on the Hanson River where they shot eight Aborigines before returning to Alice Springs. In his official report on the shootings, Murray did not mention the number of people killed in his expedition. Only later in the inquiry did he admit to killing fourteen Aborigines. In total, it was found that 'twenty and a number of others' were killed and 'shot not known whether killed ... one and a number of others.'[1] The killings were found to be justified, and the white men were exonerated.

Some years later, the stockman Walter Smith visited the Lander and described the following sight:

> *They were like paddy-melons. The skulls. A man felt sorry. There must have been two hundred of them — big ones, little ones, women, kids, everyone.[2]*

The punitive raids have become known to whites as 'the Coniston Massacre'. The women's stories testify to the extent of the suffering experienced at Wirliyajarrayi and neighbouring countries. The stories reveal the full horror of unsuspecting people gunned down while going about their daily business. The death of so many Lander Warlpiri was an assault on the social body, the scars of which are still borne today as gaps in the genealogy of landholders. The treachery of the intruders is long remembered, and when older people walk around their country they point out the sites where relatives were killed.

Rosie Nungarrayi's account tells of Murray's murderous activities at Liirlpari (Whitestone), Patirlirri (Rabbit Bore), Jangan-kurlangu (Boomerang Waterhole) and Warlawurrukurlangu.

Molly Nungarrayi describes the massacres from yet another perspective, naming Boomerang Waterhole (Jangan-kurlangu) and Jarralyku (Curlew Waterhole) on the Lander, and Yakuranji and Warranyirrtipa on the Hanson River, as other places where deaths occurred. Molly mentions 'sorry business' — the complex and prolonged mourning practices carried out on the death of a relative. During sorry business the deceased's camp is abandoned and their tracks swept from the earth. For months, sometimes years, it is prohibited to say the deceased's name or to go near their place of death. Molly also speaks of people

---

[1] Australian Archives (NT): A431; 50/2768.
[2] Quoted in Kimber, 1986:67.

fleeing the Lander area for Warumungu country to the north-east, near Tennant Creek. One can only imagine the protracted grief and dislocation set in train by the massacres.

Milly Nangala's account tells of a massacre that took place during an initiation ceremony.[3]

The Lander River in full flood, 1987.

Shooting us like bullocks

Rosie Nungarrayi

The policemen came travelling this way, north, after the shooting time. They came from Pijaraparnta. That's where they came upon a lot of people and slaughtered them, our relatives. This happened when I was a young girl.

After that, the policemen came to Liirlpari [Whitestone]. Again the policemen killed some people there. Then the policemen travelled west to Patirlirri [Rabbit Bore] looking for people. Again they killed a lot more of our people, my brother, Johnny Kitson's father. For a whole day they went around shooting at people. They shot them just like bullocks. They shot the young men coming out from bush camp where they'd been initiated. People were shot digging for rabbits in our country, Muranjayi. They were getting *yakajirri* berries, yams and *wanakiji* tomatoes. Those people they shot had nothing to do with it. The policemen shot them for nothing. Again they killed a lot of men there. No-one breathed. All were dead. Women were alive. They let the women go alive and killed the men.

After that the whitefellas went to Jangan-kurlangu [Boomerang Waterhole]. Those

---

[3] See Read and Read, 1991, and Koch, 1993, for a more detailed account of the killings at Patirlirri.

people were out hunting at Boomerang Hole when the whitefellas came for them. They were getting possum and vegetable food, and some were grinding different types of seeds to make flour. (They used to take green seeds and leave them in the sun until they were dry and then grind them.) Again the policemen killed a lot of men and left the women alone. That old woman Nakamarra witnessed this.

The whitefellas went northwards towards Yinapaka [Lake Surprise], chasing people there. They tried to catch people, but they ran away.

People travelled through Dingo Hole right up to Yinapaka. A whitefella followed their tracks to Yilyampuru, on this side of Yinapaka, and killed some in their camp. Many people didn't come back but kept on travelling northwards.

The whitefellas then travelled east to Warlawurrukurlangu, where they found Molly Napangardi's father's eldest brother, a Japanangka, who had two wives, two Napurrulas. The whitefellas sent them away and then fired after them, shooting them like dogs. Half of the men and women were shot. The wives tried to protect the men by standing in front of them and blocking the bullets, but they were shot too. My husband's father, Jampijinpa, was one of them.

After the whitefellas killed a lot of people they travelled eastward to Stirling. Napurrula and Japanangka saw them coming and ran away to Stirling. That Napurrula was from Wapilingki, in the west. Japanangka and Napurrula went to Stirling and saved their lives. The policeman, whom we called Kuluparnta [fighter], continued on to Barrow Creek. He went backwards and forwards over the same tracks, looking for people and their hiding places. Back over the tracks, looking for people who had come back after the shooting. Even then he shot more people.

They were living on wild pussycats, goanna, and different kinds of lizards. While people were digging for yarla roots they were shot by the white man. Those old people were naked, not wearing any clothes, poor things. Another group of white people were travelling from the west, bringing bullocks and wagons with them, and these people also started shooting our people. Molly and I were only young girls. We used to run away frightened when we saw the whitefellas come up. Frightened, we'd hide. We'd dig a hole in the wet sand to make ourselves cool and sleep there until dark. ❐

Fleeing into the sandhills

Molly Nungarrayi

We stayed at Tipinpa, in my country, Patirlirri. We didn't know what was happening. Later my two grandmothers came with a *yampinyi*[1] for my mother's father. My aunties, Napaljarris, saw them coming and started keening. I watched this sorry business when I was a little girl.

My two grandmothers looked after me. Whitefellas came to where we were living and surrounded us. They pointed at the smoke that my mother and father lit while out hunting. They asked, 'Who made the fire over there?' The old man replied, 'I'm the one who made the bush fire.' Then the whitefellas fired. They wounded some of my family, Napaljarri and Jakamarra, and an old Jupurrula. He still has the bullet holes in his side. After the shooting we went off to a place called Taripari. Whitefellas came looking for us everywhere with camels and horses. They found some people at Boomerang Waterhole and shot them too. Then they went to Jarralyku. People ran away, terrified. The whitefellas tried to ride up the sandhills, but their horses bogged in the sand. The people were really frightened. The whitefellas fired at our people, but they kept on running, right through Jarralyku. That's where they caught up with people and shot them, at Jarralyku. There were men and women running frightened! The people fled toward Warumungu country. Only years later did they return.

The whitefellas turned back and went straight to Yakuranji [Hanson River] and found my grandparents from Ngarnalkurru. They were getting rabbits at a place called Warranyirrtipa when my grandmother was shot. My grandfather left his wife and went to tell the others. The rabbits were still cooking in the fire! My grandfather was sorry for his wife. The whitefellas were shooting people all around that area!

There was an old man and his wife trying to protect each other. The whitefellas shot them both. Others were still alive. A whitefella forced one of the women to hit her husband. Then they went back to Mud Hut, where they looked around with camels and horses until they found other people. Some ran off and hid in the caves, others ran into the bush. My grandmother and grandfather were looking after me then. A whitefella fired at them. My mother and grandmother were coming back from hunting when they heard this shot. I also heard it, when I was a little girl. ❐

[1] *Yampinyi* is the deceased's personal belongings, which are kept in a swag. It is a symbolic focus of the mourners' grief, until such time as all parties involved have carried out their immediate responsibilities to each other in relation to the deceased.

Coming back from ceremony

Milly Nangala

My family walked from Patirlirri to Kunajarrayi, where they had ceremonial business. They sang, *Kardarrarra, kardarrarra* [a refrain chanted during ceremonies]. Celina's grandfather was with a Japaljarri. They had travelled together to the ceremony. At that time they were making young men, and the young men were coming out of the bush. The women were singing *Kardarrarra, kardarrarra* when the whitefellas came shooting. At the sound of the bullets people scattered. The young men were just coming out of the bush camp. Celina's grandfather was living at Pawu [Mount Barkly], and the Japaljarris were living at Patirlirri when the whitemen came shooting. Palarla went with them to Marliyarrawarnu, where they had sorry business. ❐

Some didn't come back

Because the Lander area had become a place of violence and death, many Lander Warlpiri fled their traditional country. Over time they settled in other areas: at Tennant Creek, at the mines at Wauchope, Barrow Creek and Hatches Creek, and near ration depots established by missions. In 1943 the Anglican missionaries Mr and Mrs Long ran a ration depot six miles from the old Tennant Creek Telegraph Station, and among the entries in the ration books were the names of Warlpiri who had fled the Lander during the 1928 massacres. When the water supply dried up, the mission was relocated to Phillip Creek and called the Manga Manda Settlement.[1] In 1955 it was moved to Warrabri (Alekarenge), the government settlement where Warlpiri, Kaytetye, Alyawarr and Warumungu people were forcibly settled under the Assimilation Policy.

Rosie Nungarrayi

When we settled down a bit after the trouble, we started to eat again. Some of the people from Yinapaka who fled north didn't come back. They ended up at the old Telegraph Station called Seven Mile, just north of Tennant Creek. Later, they went to the mission at Phillip Creek. ❐

---

[1] See Topsy Nelson Napurrula's story of the dormitory at Phillip Creek Mission in Read and Read, 1991:97–100.

After the massacres

After the slaughter on the Lander and Hanson Rivers Tilmouth headed east. Morton and Sandford stayed on at Broadmeadows, where they were joined by another white, Jimmy Wickham. The men harrassed the local inhabitants in an attempt to drive them from the Lander. The Warlpiri had little choice but to retaliate, and for a few years a state of guerilla warfare existed. So effective was Aboriginal resistance that Morton and Sandford were forced to abandon their interests in Warlpiri country.[1]

Morton returned to his block in Yanmajirri country,[2] near the Overland Telegraph Line, before moving east to take up Ammaroo Station where he was involved in yet another massacre.[3]

Wickham bought Morton and Sandford's bullocks and, on 9 June 1931, he applied for Morton and Sandford's leases on the Lander. He was granted grazing licences (GL 496 & 673) for nine hundred square miles of Warlpiri country, and named the area Willowra.[4] He set up base camps on the Lander at Wirliyajarrayi (the site of Willowra community today), at Warlawurrukurlangu and Yardingurnangu. Wickham employed a white stockman called Bob Davis to help him with his cattle operation. Davis was married to Morton's sister.

Over the next few years a small number of white prospectors passed through Willowra in search of gold. Among them was Harold A. Waldron, who met his death in suspicious circumstances whilst camped with three other prospectors at Munyupanji. At this place, called Waldron's Hill in English, Waldron lies buried today.[5] One suggestion is that the person referred to as Walter in the following account was Waldron, but this seems unlikely.

The following stories deal with women's memories of life on the Lander River in the decade after the 1928 massacres.

---

[1] See Terry, 1931:217, note.

[2] Later to become Anningie Station.

[3] According to Territory pioneer Kurt Johannsen, Morton and his mate Murray killed over a hundred Aborigines on the Sandover River in retribution for cattle killing (Johannsen, 1992:66).

[4] Australian Archives (NT): F630; PL 373.

[5] R. D. (Doug) Cooper, an employee of Waldron, claimed that Waldron had caught his foot in the stirrup of a horse, which then bolted, dragging and kicking the rider to death (Australian Archives [NT]: A1; Item 1937 14097). Local history has it that Waldron was killed by whites, and his death made to look like an accident.

Hiding from those with no human feelings

In telling how families looked out for each other during this period, Molly Nungarrayi con-
trasts Warlpiri humanity with that of whites, describing the latter as 'people with no
human feelings.' She tells of the terror people lived with as they travelled through the coun-
try in search of food and water. Molly recounts how a number of families from neighbour-
ing areas had to flee for their lives, to Warumungu country in the east. Not wanting to
leave their homeland, yet afraid of attracting unwanted attention, Molly's family lay low
in the spinifex country, where they temporarily abandoned important cultural practices
such as sorry business. Things quietened down during the war years, and people were able
to move around freely once more. Molly talks about some of the changes introduced by the
army, and how the coming of the Parkinson family to Willowra ushered in a new era of
Aboriginal/European relations.

Molly Nungarrayi

After my mother's burial I tried to talk for her and finish the sorry business, but my aunty,
Napaljarri, told me, 'You mob sort out the trouble, that's your business. We are not going to
join you, because the whitefellas are walking around with horses and rifles everywhere.'
We were all walking around together, all the family sticking together so that no-one would
get killed. We didn't go to other places. We were frightened of whitefellas. We were hiding
in places around Ngarnalkurru, your place.[1] We lived in that direction, not far away. We
did not run away frightened. Our parents stayed here all the time, Japanangka and
Japaljarri.

We used to hide quietly in the thick bush or out in the spinifex. We ate meat in the bush
and spinifex country where no-one would find us. We used to come for water in the late
afternoon and go back to the spinifex at night. Our parents took us to hide in the spinifex
country. The Nakamarras used to take their children, they took them quietly to their
fathers. They built shelters for us to sleep in.

Well, we lay down then in the roots of the tree, in the gaps in the rock and under rocky
ledges. Once after a sleep we saw an emu standing near us, peeping in at us, until my father
came to get water in the creek. When the sun shone on us we lay covered by the cool sand.
Our parents ran to get water at the waterhole near the bloodwood trees. Although they
were frightened, some used to hunt out in the open sun.

Some relatives came from other places. We used to embrace each other when the families gathered together. We used to travel around here, not far away. Other people were
scared of the white man and fled to other places, but not my family. We stayed here,
around here, near Patirlirri, Ngarnalkurru and to the west, to Taripari. We did not disap-
pear when there was trouble.

Well, later we went east to Wajirrkinyanu, we weren't here. But we only went on a holiday to visit family. We came back here with our family, Japaljarri and Japanangka. We were
living without fear now. It was quieter. In other places, some distance away, people were

---

[1] Here Molly is talking to Petronella Vaarzon-Morel. Ngarnalkurru is the country with which the latter is closely
    identified.

driven off the open spaces with bullets and rifles by those who had no human feelings. They could not hide from that. No. It seemed they were shot as far away as Warumungu country, far away where we could not see what was going on. Far away on the Yanmajirri side they were being shot, but we could not tell what was happening.

Well, as for us, we had our education here in our own home, in the old days. We grew up learning the old ways. Japanangka and Japaljarri gathered us together and took us with them. They had grown old and sick during the time that they were travelling around hiding. The old women had trouble too. We were feeling all right staying here then. The trouble had gone.

We ate *yawakiyi* [bush plums] and conkerberries and we dug for yams. It was only later that we saw flour, when the army was there. That's the time that we ate flour, in Parkinsons' time. We started cooking damper when the army started, then we came back to Willowra. We used to taste it now and then when Wickham was here first.

After the trouble ended and we could move around freely, we went east. We travelled all around. It was during army time at New Barrow that we cooked flour and other things that came this way. We started getting flour during the time of the army, the time of the important soldiers. In our own country we travelled around gathering and eating conkerberries and yams.

It was when we went over to the army at New Barrow that we began to eat flour. We ate and ate. There was now plenty of flour and bread. We still did not know how to make bread. Later we learnt how to cook it in the way that it was done at the army depot.

We turned around and came back here. Mr Parkinson was here. He became a good friend. It was during his time that we stayed here without any more trouble, with our own space to move around in. It was during the time of the army that clothes came. In Wickham's time we were always hiding, and in Parkinson's time we moved around freely. Jampijinpa and Jungarrayi joined the army. Lots of people were going to join the army. Free time. That was a long time ago. ❐

Kathy Nangala with **rdajalpa** *(children's python), 1988.*

How we hid when I was a girl

In the following oral history, Nungarrayi describes some of the strategies people used to resist the whites. She recounts how children were hidden during the day while their parents hunted for food. Afraid of being sighted in daylight, they waited until nightfall before creeping down to the waterholes for water.

Nungarrayi

When the whitefellas first came to our country a long time ago, they started shooting our people. They shot some dead, and chased others away from their land so that they never returned. The whitefellas chased people from places like Yinapaka, Yilyampuru, Jarralyku and Kunajarrayi. My poor people were chased off their country for ever. They went to places like Tennant Creek and Phillip Creek.

When I was a little girl I saw my people shot at — all because they lived off this country and because they were Aborigines. Some of our parents and grandparents hid us in caves. During the day we'd go without water and hide from the whitefellas. At night our parents would sneak out to the soakages to get water for us to drink. They would leave us little ones in the caves for an hour or two and we'd cry, wondering when they'd return. We were frightened. We knew the whitefellas were after us and could shoot us. But they didn't. Our parents came back carrying water in a large wooden container that they'd put grass around the edges of, to stop the water spilling out. They'd come back to us and say, 'You little ones are still here?', and we'd answer back, 'Yes, we're still here, alive.' Sometimes they'd pour water on our heads to keep us cool. After drinking the water we'd sleep.

We stayed there for a week or two, then we left the cave for another place. We went further and further away from the whitefellas. As we travelled our parents and grandparents hunted meat. They gathered berries and roots, and ground seeds for us to eat. We used to look around to see if there were any whites coming before we went out. During the hot weather we'd tie our feet with vines and grass to protect them from the hot sand. We'd put leafy branches on top of our heads to shade us from the burning sun. Nowadays we buy things from the shop, but at that time we were bone naked, poor things. No boots. We didn't have any clothes at that time. No pubic tassels. We were just naked little girls.

Later the whitefellas went back to where they'd come from and we started going back to the country where we were born. All the way back to our country we found people who had been shot and we mourned them. That is how most of us lived. We left our country because of the cruel whitefellas and their guns. Most of us were lucky, for the whitefellas never saw us. ❐

Staying in our country

Rosie Nungarrayi describes how some older Warlpiri used sorcery to protect themselves from the whites who rode around terrorising them. In the first incident, an old Japaljarri sang his attacker's rifle so that the trigger jammed. In the second, a powerful old Napaljarri sang the bullets of her attacker so that they fell away when he fired. In describing the thuggish treatment meted out by whites to the Aborigines, Rosie says that it was 'just like they were rounding up bullocks.'

Rosie Nungarrayi

When we settled down after the shooting business we went out hunting. Whitefellas were still in our country. Once a whitefella came across my father digging for rabbits. Old Japaljarri used his water carrier as a shield to protect himself from the bullets, while another Japaljarri, his older brother, sang the bullets. One dog was shot in the ears. We [Molly and Rosie] were standing nearby, watching the old men. We thought, 'What is he waiting for?' That Japaljarri, the eldest brother, sang the rifle. The whitefella pointed the rifle at old Japaljarri and pulled the trigger. It didn't go off! The trigger was stuck because the Japaljarri had sung the rifle to save his brother, who only had a water carrier for a shield. Those bullets were wasted. Not one of the bullets hit the old man.

That whitefella left to get more powder for the bullets. He went to Sandford Bore from Mud Hut. We two Nungarrayis and our fathers ran away. The whitefella produced more bullets and then returned to Mud Hut, but we had gone to Wirliyajarrayi. He didn't find us, but he smashed our grinding stones in two, and he burnt our bough shade and all our possessions. All finished. But we were safe.

Nugget Morton was still living at Mud Hut at this time. Bob Davis and Wickham lived together here at Wirliyajarrayi, with a man called Walter. Three whitefellas. They used to put grass between their teeth when they went out shooting Aboriginal people. Those three used to run together. They rode westward shooting at more people. They used to travel on horses around Pirlimanu. They searched for people around every soakage, following their tracks.

At one of the soakages an old Napaljarri struck Bob Davis on his neck with a yam stick. She sang all his bullets, and they fell out onto the ground. But those three whitefellas still looked for more people. After the rain the people would dig for yams. That's when the whitefellas fired at them, while they were digging for food. After rain they always went hunting for food away from the main waterholes, and those three men would track them down.

They'd see smoke rising from the people's fires and gallop after them. People fired grass to force the animals out. They didn't know that people were out hunting them. My family heard the sound of horses galloping and saw birds flying out of trees. The whitefellas followed their footprints down to the soakages, but by the time they got there the people had gone. The whitefellas followed the tracks at soakages. They rode with two men on the side and another in the middle — just like they were rounding up bullocks. ❐

Still trying to force us out

Nungarrayi expresses the outrage people felt at being forced out of their own country. However, despite the brutality of the whites, many people refused to leave their homeland.

Nungarrayi

Whitefellas came around and took over our country. They were in our country. We had made bough shelters for ourselves, and Nungarrayi made a shelter for Jangala, who had been speared, when we heard a gun shot. A whitefella followed the smoke we made by firing the grass for rabbits. We could see him coming with a horse and a rifle. 'What will we do?' we said. 'Where did that whitefella come from?' A dog chased the whitefella on the horse and the whitefella shot it. I saw him shoot the dog. He fired at people when they shouted at him. They cried out as they were shot and fell down. Nungarrayi cried out for some people to help her with Jangala. He couldn't run, he was crippled. 'You mob go away,' the whitefella shouted. 'You can live out in the bush but don't come back here.' Still the people came back.

My family came back to Willowra and we met up with whitefellas. They came back from Liirlpari. Betsy Nampijinpa and her mother fired the grass for rabbits, and I fired a patch to clear it to dig yams. I went off as the sun went down and came back with a container full of onions. I thought I heard a gunshot. I told one of the women, but they said, 'No, that's only the grass crackling from the bushfire.' I said, 'I heard a gunshot coming from the south.' Then we saw the whitefella coming, following people's tracks.

I ran off with my mother. We were frightened. That whitefella saw me run to my dog and bend over to hide it. I left my onions and digging stick in the shade and ran to save my dog. My mother shouted, 'Let that dog go, or he'll hit me instead of the dog.' The old people were forcing one of the old men to sing the bullets. The whitefella said to the old man, 'Eh, what are you doing with your mouth?' The old man replied, 'It's just that my lips are a bit dry.' He went on singing and the whitefella again asked him what he was doing, and the old man replied, 'I'm frightened of you, I want to run away.' The whitefella tried to shoot them but he couldn't. The gun just went click, click. That old man had sung the gun. Everyone started to run away. The whitefella ran to the bough shade and picked up a digging stick, but instead of hitting me, he hit the dog under the blanket. The dog ran out from the blanket, howling. 'All right you mob, go west and don't come back to this place or this way again,' he growled at us.

We packed all our things and left. When I picked up my container, the whitefella grabbed it, threw the onions away and smashed it. He broke my digging stick in two with his boots. The boomerangs and the spears that were covered by the sand, he broke these too. He told me to throw my blanket down to the ground, but I told him that I was going to take it. We went west, and I climbed a tree and watched the whitefella burn our camp. I saw him travelling north then, so we returned to our camp, to that same place. When we arrived back we began calling out for the dogs, which had run off hiding into the bush, and they came back. Our dogs were still alive. We stayed there for a long time in the Liirlpari area, at a place called Ngantinkipinkirla. 'Don't make any more bushfires,' we said to each other. That whitefella went everywhere looking for Aboriginal people. ❐

More whitefellas and cattle

In the following account, Rosie Nungarrayi recalls some of the different white men who came into her country during the period from the late 1920s to the late 1940s. First there was Nugget Morton, who committed various atrocities against Warlpiri people in an attempt to drive them from the country. It was during Morton's time at Willowra that Brookes was killed at Yurrkuru (Brookes Soak). Some time later, cattle were driven up the Lander by a group of white men and Aborigines from the north-west. Rosie particularly remembers a Warringari woman they called Kardunyngali. Wickham then arrived at Willowra and, after initially harrassing the Warlpiri, he settled down, giving rations to Aborigines in return for work. Wickham stayed until Parkinson took over in 1946.

Rosie Nungarrayi

It was just before the camels came here that old Japanangka hit the whitefella. Later, when Wickham settled down, people worked for him in return for bullock fat and beef water. We used to dip our fingers in this mixture and lick them. This was in the olden times. Wickham left Mud Hut and settled down at Wirliyajarrayi [Willowra]. Nugget Morton lived at Boomerang Waterhole. Other people came from the west with bullocks and they brought an Aboriginal woman with them. This new group were Warringari people from Western Australia, Mutpurra, and white men. This was the time we started eating beef.

One Nampijinpa, a Warringari woman called Kardunyngali and a lot of European men brought bullocks from Western Australia. They followed the little creeks until they arrived

*Nampijinpa fashions a **kuturu** from mulga wood.*

at Boomerang Waterhole and then went on to Yinapaka. We Warlpiri only wore pubic tassels. It was after the whitefellas came from Western Australia that people began wearing clothes. Before this time, when they dug for yams, they didn't wear clothes. We two Nungarrayis used to walk around naked. No clothes. It was after these whitefellas that we began to wear clothes. This was after they finished shooting people. The good whitefellas gave us clothes.

The people began getting bullocks from Wickham. They were still shooting at people at this time. One fight started when someone killed a cat. They didn't know it belonged to the whitefella, Nugget Morton. He followed people's tracks and fired at them again. Old Jampijinpa and Japanangka ran away. Because Anne Napanangka's grandfather had died and an old Jampijinpa had passed away at Ti Tree, the Napurrulas cut their hair for sorry business. Nugget Morton asked the women why their hair was cut, and then hit them on the head — just because of that pussycat.

Nugget Morton attacked many Ngarnalkurru people. Celina's grandmother and her grandmother's daughter were shot. Nugget Morton shot at the whole lot, Japanangka, Napurrula, Napangardi and Japangardi when they were hunting for witchetty grubs at Rdajirdaji soakage. Another group were safe. These Japaljarris, their wives, Nakamarras, and their in-laws used to go out at night to drink water. They hid far away from Ngarnalkurru. They lived in the Mount Barkly hills and moved around and around that country, in one place.

Every night they used to drink water from the soakage. After rain fell they shifted out into the bush, to new soakages further away. When the creek flooded and the soakages were full of water, there was plenty of food. Nugget Morton was the last whitefella left shooting at Aboriginal people. Some people from Western Australia were still here, and Kardunyngali, the Aboriginal woman. ❐

Life goes on

The following three stories recount aspects of life in the 1930s and early 1940s, during Wickham's time. Essentially, Lander Warlpiri still led a hunter-gatherer life, albeit circumscribed by the presence of Wickham and his cronies. Not only did Warlpiri have to endure harrassment by the petty tyrants, but their major waterholes continued to be occupied by whites and their country eaten out by cattle. The Warlpiri retaliated at every opportunity.

Nungarrayi

People gathered together at Liirlpari [Whitestone], to the south. They began a ceremony for everyone and caught the boys, to make them young men. There was a fight after the dancing finished. It was in the afternoon. They used spears, boomerangs, stone knives. An old Japaljarri speared a Jangala with a shovel-nosed spear. It was afternoon when they were fighting. There was a lot of bush food at that place, *yakajirri* berries, *yirrakurru* onions, and seeds. A big star fell down near that place.

After it was over they travelled northwards. Old Jakamarra went around with Jupurrula. Father and son travelled to the south and took the young men back home after the ceremonies. All the Nungarrayis travelled north, to Ngapatura soakage, and stayed there for one night. That old Jupurrula stayed there with them, and then they went on to Jinpa. From Jinpa they travelled to Kurrurdurdu. An old Jampijinpa passed away there, so they went to Ngarntajariwana where they painted themselves for sorry business. Then they came to Kajuru, where they stayed for a little while, then went to Nyinjirri and Yinirntiparnta. They camped at these soakages at night. In the morning they caught rabbits by burning off the grass to force the animals out. They didn't know that whitefellas were around. ❐

Lucy Nampijinpa

We ate *wakirlpirri* beans and walked around naked, no clothes. We used to play around when we were little kids and hit each other. Our mothers used to say, 'Don't you mob fight, we are far away from water.' They had to get water in wooden containers. They used to go out for yams, yakajirri berries, pussycat and goannas. This was at Liirlpari, Kajuru and Wilypatiparnta. We used to walk around and come back to those same places. They used to dig water from the soakages in the creek. Nangala told us, 'Go down there, you children, there's some water there for you to drink.' Our mothers and aunties poured water into the water carriers. The Nungarrayis, our mothers, told us, 'Stay in one place, don't wander off, because the whitefella might see you.'

Lady Nampijinpa fashions a crowbar. First the end of the crowbar is heated in a flour drum and then the end is pounded into shape with the back of a tomahawk.

Wickham was still here.

Our mothers used to look for *wakirlpirri* beans and *pirlarla* seeds that fell from the trees near the windbreaks. Then they ground them for us kids. We used to wait for our mothers to come back from hunting in the late afternoon. They'd bring back yakajirri berries, goanna, and yams. While they were out hunting, the mothers worried about their children, saying, 'We must go home.' They filled the water containers until they were full and brought them back for us kids. They carried some with them hunting.

We used to shout out, 'There's Mummy coming back with lots of food from hunting.' They'd come back with cooked meat and give us *wanakiji* tomatoes and *yakajirri* berries. We ate it all, the cooked meat and the vegetable food. We didn't fight with one another but were really good. We used to stay in the creek at Wilypatiparnta and Kajuru with our families.

When we grew bigger we saw Wickham. He came in our direction and saw us. We were naked with no clothes. He came and asked us children, 'Where have your mothers gone?' We had no clothes. We sat in the shade like birds. He talked to us, but we

Gwendolyn carries a bark container of honey and **yakajirri** *berries gathered by Nampijinpa.*

didn't answer him, we just watched him. We sat very quiet. 'You kids go over there to the tea-tree bushes,' he shouted. We ran over there and hid behind the bushes, hugging each other, frightened. He took out matches and then burnt down our shade shelters. Then he saw the soakage and trampled all over it with his horse, filling it in. Our mothers were wondering what was happening to us back home. They thought, 'Oh, the whitefella may have found them there.' Wickham smashed the grinding stones and wax to pieces. He threw the axes down and broke them in two. This happened in the olden days. ❐

Molly Nungarrayi

In Wickham's time we used to sneak around walking. We used to get tea, flour and beef — through the bushes, sneaking. We used to walk around and get tucker, our fathers, mothers and my sisters and me. We used to all meet up at a little place, Kajuru, to the west. We used to get rations in Wickham's time. That's the first time we tasted flour, tea and beef.

We used to live with a few Japaljarris. We stayed there, eating our rations. We used to get rations, sneaking, stealing, with the Japaljarris. Three Nakamarras and three Japaljarris. We used to take the rations back to Kajuru. We stayed there and then went looking for bush food. We used to go out from Kajuru and walk around hunting. We used to eat, eat, eat. We used to sneak around and get tucker in Wickham's time. After that we travelled through Ngarnalkurru and collected yams and killed rabbits. We used to kill snakes and eat them at Yurnturrkunyu. We used to get onion bulbs, rabbits and possum and cook and eat them. All the Nakamarras used to take us around to hunt with them. This was in Wickham's time. After this we used to come back, but we didn't go through Wirliyajarrayi, because Wickham was violent. We used to stay at Kajuru at one place, near the creek where there was lots of water. From Kajuru we went east to Mount Peake, and then we'd come back to the same place.

Bob Davis, Walter and Wickham used to go round shooting with guns for rabbits. They'd go around poking at all the coolamons, grinding stones, baby carriers and seed containers, and smash them up. They'd chuck them away. We'd keep clear of Wickham. We were frightened, but we'd go back to that same place again. At night we used to come out, hiding. We'd take the rations back to camp, and we'd eat, eat, eat. ❐

Milly Nangala

They used to steal food every night from Wickham's camp. As the sun went down, he'd saddle his horse and go looking for the women's tracks and follow them to the camps. Wickham said to Lucy's grandmother, 'You're the one who stole my axe!' 'Hit me then,' said old Nakamarra. He slapped her face with his hand. I said, 'Grab that rifle from him and throw it into the water.' I forced two women to sing the rifle. Old Nakamarra sang Wickham's gun. He pointed the gun towards her, but it didn't go off, because it was sung. ❐

Working as 'stockmen'

The first Aborigines to work for the whites at Willowra were women. They did stockwork and domestic chores in exchange for rations. Some became the sexual partners of the men. At the time, it was illegal for single white men to employ Aboriginal women or to marry an Aboriginal woman without permission.[1]

Although the whites discouraged visits from the women's relatives, the women passed on information, rations and goods, such as axes and knives, to their kin. One of the 'stockmen' was Kitty Kitson Napangardi, of Yanmajirri and Afghan descent. Recruited as a young girl, Kitty worked as a horsetailer and stockman for Wickham. Because of her Yanmajirri ancestry, Kitty was regarded as a relation of people at Willowra, and could thus be called upon to provide goods. In the following two extracts, Milly Nangala and Rosie Nungarrayi recount how they obtained goods from Kitty and from other women employed by Wickham.

Milly Nangala

Kitty Napangardi was a stockman, horsetailer for Wickham. There used to be a yard behind the school, near the bloodwood tree, where they broke the colts in. In those times it was the girls who broke the horses in. I used to watch the women breaking in the colts. Wickham told me, 'You go away, you're too small to be here.'

One day, when Kitty was drinking tea, I came up to Wickham's camp. Kitty saw me standing there and asked, 'What did you come for?' I told her, 'I came for food and tobacco, I'm the only person who came, I came because I have no meat or flour.' I used to visit Kitty's camp every lunchtime. I was the only one that Wickham allowed to come. We were thinking about axes: 'Who is going to give us axes?' We used them to cut trees. Also Kitty Napurrula, two Napangardis and one Nangala used to give flour, golden syrup, bullock meat, soap, tobacco and sugar to the other women. ❐

Rosie Nungarrayi

Every night we'd get meat from Wickham. He lived down near the creek, and old Ngipirdiya Nangala was there too. We'd get meat from Kitty Napurrula. She'd give us flour, and we'd go hunting for bush food. We'd come back in the afternoon, hiding in the shade, afraid of Wickham. ❐

---

[1] See *Born in the Cattle* for an analysis of the role of Aboriginal women in the cattle industry (McGrath, 1987).

Still dreaming about horses: Kitty Napangardi, stockwoman

Kitty loved her work. She was so skilled that she virtually ran the cattle operation. Heavily relied on by Wickham and Davis, she was treated well. At the same time, she developed enduring bonds with local women (in particular, Milly Nangala and Rosie Nungarrayi) and made sure they had access to the white man's goods. Because of Kitty's background, she had no promised husband on hand to claim her. Kitty's activities would have been unusual for a white woman at the time, but they also crossed gender lines in Warlpiri society: she hunted kangaroo, for example. Despite the fact that the Commonwealth Ordinance of 1911 had made it illegal for Aboriginal women to wear men's clothing in the company of whites, Kitty was dressed in stockmen's clothing. Here Kitty tells with pride of her experiences as a stockman. She recalls with much amusement how Warlpiri men began to learn stockwork and how to ride horses. Aboriginal men eventually replaced women as stockworkers during the 1940s.

*Kitty Napangardi and **wirrkali** tree on the site of the old horse yard, next to the Willowra school. It was here, during the 1940s, that she corralled the horses which were used for mustering cattle.*

Kitty Napangardi

ABORIGINAL ENGLISH	STANDARD ENGLISH

Little girl I bin. Well I bin start longa horses, ridem about. Eight Mile first. After that one mefella bin longa Mud Hut — Mud Hut mefella bin start. Bobs Well. After that one, Florry Well, 'nother side. Mefella cut timber, makem yard. Yardem up horses. After that one, bin wagon. 'Nother mob. I bin takem plant — horses. After that one mefella bin camp out at a big waterhole. After that one — what that jump-up

I was a little girl when I started riding horses. I used to ride them around. I'd go to Eight Mile first, and then we'd go to Mud Hut, on to Bobs Well and then to Florry Well, in the other direction. We cut timber, made a yard, and yarded the horses.[1] Later some other people brought a wagon up. We looked after the horse plant. We used to camp out at a big waterhole. We mustered horses and bullocks at Jump Up Yard,[2] in

---

[1] 'We' refers to the other stockwomen Kitty worked with.
[2] A jump up is a hill rise. Jump Up Yard is near Willowra (see photo on page 63).

Ngarnalkurru side? Well, mefella bin chasem-bout there — horses and bullock. Musterin' there. Yardem up.

Chasem up. Twofella bin start there, come back Eight Mile. Musterem up there. One horse bin buck there — horse that brumby one, you know? I bin gettem same again mine. Mine bin buck hard — talk about bullock all over the place! I bin hold-em. I bin hang on, nothing. He bin try, that horse, longa me. I bin roundem again, that bullock. Now doin' calf. Cuttem out and sendem — sendem bullock Alice.

Right. Through yard, 'nother side of — this side of what's-a-name? Eight Mile. And Juju yard been there, eh? That's mefel-la bin makem. Puttin' like that — timber, you know. Post. Cuttem open them, pressem in, puttem them. Mefella bin yar-dem there, somefella. I worked every day — Juju yard, this side, longa mulga, you know [indicating the south]. All right. *Yali* [just over there]. Allabout bin broke one. Rabbit bin run — no yard and all. Bin put-tem bore. Well mefella bin chasem round outside now. I bin hold 'nother lot. That 'nother dead fella — twofella bin holdem 'nother one again. *Karnta* mob.

I worked for Bob Davis and that two men — not boss one, old Wickham. Him never look afterem — only Bob Davis bin help. Right. Mefella bin mixem that mob. I went to gettem horse. Morning you know. Saddlem. 'Nother mob bin go gettem bul-lock. Me bin come — plant horse behind, and wagon there [laughter].

All right. Mefella bin come Mud Hut now. Mustering about there — Mud Hut and plain, you know — that side. Mefella bin roundem there now, all night. And big rain bin come. No coat — only trousers and shirt. And shoes and hat, that's all. Handkerchief, gloves, I think. Use-em this [indicating how gloves are slipped on the hands]. I use-em-bout cuttem that one

the Ngarnalkurru area.

We mustered them there, then returned to Eight Mile where we'd muster some more. One of the wild horses bucked there. I rode a wild one and it bucked really hard. There were cattle everywhere. I held the horse, hanging on. He kept trying to buck me, but I held on. We'd start mustering again, separating the young calves from the bullocks, and then send the bullocks to Alice.

We mustered the cattle bringing them to Juju Yard at Eight Mile. We made that yard. We cut the timber and then put the posts in the ground. We yarded the cattle. I worked every day at Juju Yard. It's in the south, near the mulga trees. That yard's broken now, the rabbits are running around, and they've put a bore there. We chased cattle outside of that yard. I held one lot while another two women rounded up the others.

I worked for those two men, Bob Davis and Wickham. Wickham never worked with the cattle, only Bob Davis helped. In the morning I'd go and get my horse and saddle it. One lot of people would go out to muster the bullocks, and I'd bring the plant of horses up behind them. There was a wagon there.

All right. I'd go to Mud Hut then. Once we were mustering around the plain at Mud Hut, working at night, when a big storm came. I didn't have any coat, only trousers and shirt, and shoes, hat, handker-chief and gloves. I wore the gloves with the tops of the fingers cut off so that I could hold the bridle. We brought the horses up to Sandford Well and looked after them

The old yards at Jump Up, 1988.

[showing how the tops of the fingers of the gloves were cut off to allow for greater movement of the hands], one each again. You gotta holdem that bridle eh? That's all, nothing here. Right, mefella bin bringem that horse. Ooh, mefella bin havem longa Sandford Well. Sandford mefella bin watchem-bout there. Come up this way you know. Big yard bin longa that school eh? Yard, that's all.

Right. Right. Bringem here, yardem here now. And somefella bin come up, you know. Killem that bullock. Get 'nother mob now. Men and all. Men gotta go. Me bin all day stop now. Mefella now. Two whitefella gone, Mrs Davis too. One missus, poor bugger. Twofella bin livin' there [pointing to the present office area] in house made of — what's name now? Bushes. That lady bin waitin'. Twofella bin go gettem truck. Well I bin all day — all bin get in long Alice — I bin do behind. I bin gettem camel and working, you know, bore. Look round engine, you know. Right. I bin go longa Mud Hut to Sandford. After that one I bin come back, Mud Hut now. And allabout all right. And fillem up diesoline, you know.

there. Then we'd come back this way [to Willowra]. There used to be a big yard where that school is now.

I'd bring some cattle up here to the yards for some men to kill for meat. They got another mob then, men and all. Then I'd get more. I'd stop here, looking after the cattle, when Bob Davis and his poor wife, Mrs Davis, left. Only one white woman on her own, poor thing. She used to live over there [pointing to the site of the station office], in a house made of bushes.

Mrs Davis waited behind when Bob Davis and Wickham went to pick up a truck in Alice. I stayed here and worked, with camels, looking after the engine [for the windmills]. I'd go and fill the engines up with diesoline at Mud Hut and Sandford [Bore]. There were other people working back here [at Willowra] then.

Me be all day start engine — whole lot of 'em. 'Nother mob bin here [laughter].

Yeah, I bin all day go. Right. Come back. One windmill bin here. Right. That Mrs Davis bin all day bringem ration — everything, sugar, everything, tea, tobacco. Oh, fullup. He bin all day bringem. Loadem up there again. Yeah. And clothes *ngalipa-nyangu* [ours]. Trousers and shirt. No dress.

Other Aboriginal people living long Mount Barkly. And Wirntijangu somefella. And near Tipinpa. Only visiting all day come, that what's-a-name? Molly. Molly bin a young girl, poor bugger — and Ruth too. Not that fat one. Young girls now, that twofella. And Nungarrayi skinny one — today him bin get fat. His daughter — and Lucy, little kid bin, young girl — Ruth bin gottem that one. Big Nungarrayi you know, Molly had nothing yet. That never givit, you know, ration everyday. And that Milly Nangala, him bin young. Him bin all day hold him about one kid, Margaret.

Mefella all day bin givit tobacco — what allabout bin wantem. And tucker — bullock, *kuyu* [meat], and flour a little. For visitor. And that *nganayi* [what's-her-name] too, Minnie. Him bin young girl. And two kids play — same as that one. Him bin all day come here. Givit ration longa him — tea and sugar. Him bin all day go back again. Anningie way, you know. Tea and sugar and ration again. You know sugar, little bit, and flour [much laughter]. And tobacco, and *kuyu, kuyu* bullock. And flour *wita* [small amount]. Him bin all day go, this one, Mount Peake way. Right, whitefella bin bringem clothes, you know. Whole lot again. Some me. Boot, belt, snake belt again — mine one [laughter]. Might be blue or olden trousers and shirt. All in blue.[3]

I'd go out every day and then come back. There was a windmill here. Every day Mrs Davis would bring me rations, everything. Sugar, tea, tobacco, lots of food and trousers and shirts for us. We didn't have dresses.

There were other Aboriginal people living at Mount Barkly, and some were at Wirntijangu, and others near Tipinpa. Ruth [Rosie Nungarrayi] and Molly visited me during the day [i.e. they didn't live around here]. They were thin young girls then, not fat like they are now. Rosie's daughter Lucy was a little kid. Milly Nangala was a young girl then, and she used to look after one kid, Margaret.

They didn't get rations. We used to give them tobacco and whatever they wanted, food, meat, and some flour. Because they were visitors. Minnie was a young kid then, playing around with Nora [her sister]. They'd come and visit, and I'd give them some tea and sugar, and then they'd leave, going back east to Anningie way. I'd give them a little bit of sugar, tea, tobacco and meat, and some flour. They'd come up all the time from Mount Peake way. Right, the whitefellas brought some clothes — some were for me — boots, a snake belt, and some olden time blue trousers and shirts.[3]

---

[3] The clothes were washed with Reckitt's Blue.

And all myall now. Not 'nother mob. That's all. That two men all day tellem. Me bin all day chasem brumby. Me and dead fella again. Gottem dinner, me bin all day go. I bin go what's-a-name? What that *nganayi* [what's that thing]? Wirntijangu — Wirntijangu [laughter]. Horses bin there, wild bugger too. Mintwofella bin hit too, longa that billabong. Mintwofella bin have-em dinner there. Me and you go look there. Might be allabout donkey this one. Right, mintwofella bin go, 'Eh, there all about.' Talk about horses bin all day buck mefella. I bin all day chasem back here.

I bin plantem some fella horses. And after that one, I start holdem them. Put them on rope — put the what's-a-name — saddle and hobble. He can't run, that one now. Take-em round, take-em round. Him all right now. I bin all day puttem bridle. Saddle up. Me bin all day ridem longa that yard. After that one, which way? Him bin all day go job, this one again, longa that creek, eh. Openem gate, shhhh. I bin use-em that one, crack. Oh, talk about 'em buck, buck, buck — nothing. I bin just put-tem quiet. I wasn't frightened. No, him bin used to 'em. All right, run around now. I bin use-em longa bullock now. Chasem 'bout. I bin all day get killer. Camp out. I bin just pickem up and bringem here. Old fella bin shootem here. Skin him back now. *Walypali,* that man, poor bugger — twofella him die. And Mrs Davis bin all day cookem bread. Him bin young here. Two of them — same one, Bob Davis and Mrs Davis. And old fella Wickham can't see — blind one. Him bin boss longa this place.

Yeah, well mefella bin come now — lit-tle one, little one, you know. Me first he bin growem up. After that — Bob Davis now, him bin livin' longa him [laughter]. Right, he bin go gettem Mrs Davis, and married. Nugget's sister. Him bin marry-em that Bob Davis now — that's his husband now.

The other Aborigines here were all *myall*, but not the workers. The white bosses told us what to do. I'd chase the brumby horses, me and another lady who is dead now. I'd get my dinner and go out for the day to Wirntijangu. There were really wild horses there. We were both hit by them, near that waterhole. The two of us had been having dinner and then went to look at what we thought might have been donkeys. Oh, everywhere! Talk about horses bucking us two! I'd chase them back here.

I'd break in some of the horses. I'd put a horse in the yard, put a rope on him, then the saddle and a hobble. He couldn't run then. I'd take him around slowly. He'd be quiet then. It could take all day to put the bridle on. Then I'd saddle up and ride him around the yard. Then what? This job went on for a long time, near the creek. Then he'd be ready to work. I'd open the gate up, cracking the whip. Talk about him buck, buck, buck! But I'd quieten him down. I wasn't frightened. I was used to it. I'd use him to muster the bullocks. I'd go out and chase up a bullock. I'd camp out. I'd pick one out and bring him back here to be killed. That old whitefella would shoot him and skin him. Poor bugger, they're both dead now. Mrs Davis always used to cook bread. She was young at the time. The two of them were Bob Davis and Mrs Davis. Wickham was an old man, and going blind. He was the boss here.

Yes, well, we came up here when we were little, little ones you know. I was the first one Wickham brought up. Then Bob Davis. He used to live with one of the Aboriginal women until he went and got Mrs Davis, Nugget's sister, and brought her back here. She married Bob Davis and he

I grew up with that twofella now. Growem longa horses. What mefella gotta do? I bin all day chasem, breakem horses. Bob Davis same again.

Me still dreamin' longa horses.

PVM: Junga? *[True?]*

KN: Yeah, every day [laughter]. Yeah, yeah. 'Nother day I bin ridem-bout, poor bugger — with cows, you know. Me ridem-about. Can't run. Everyday mefella bin all come back dinner. Ridem all day. Knock off time, come back and takem off saddle then.

And gate bin there, lettem go longa creek. He can buck, him like want to buck everyway. Tired [laughter]. Run around there again, run around there, everywhere, come back. Lettem go now. 'Nother one, 'nother one now. Like that mefella bin do, me bin all day do-em. Not 'nother two.

And man bin come up, you know. What's-a-name that, who that what's-a-name? Tom Rawlins bin here. After that one — him bin go back — Jack Long bin here now. Him bin bringin' boy. Oh, that horses mob bin eatem up allabout no-savvy man, you know. Girl him bin know. Talk about buck jump! Everyway [laughter]! Ey, you know that tree there — *wirrkali* — I bin tellem you? Tinti-tinti? That horse bin come out there. And him bin two throw there — bucking. And that — arse over, that man bin. Poor thing, *warringiyi,* Janet's father — that Napanangka.

GN: Warringiyi purdangka? *[Grandfather?]*

KN: Yeah, that one now horse bin chuckem that one. Woke-em up. Tinti-tinti. Finish him. Talk about swell-up, this one!

was her husband now.

I grew up with those two, growing up with the horses, learning about stockwork. I'd chase the horses and break them in. Bob Davis worked with me.

I still dream about those horses.

PVM: Is that true?

KN: Yes, every day. At other times I'd ride the horses slowly, mustering cattle. I'd ride them about. Every day we'd come back for dinner; we'd ride them. At knock-off time we'd come back and take the saddle off.

I'd let them go in that paddock near the creek, and they'd run around for a while. I'd take a fresh one, work it, and then let it go like the others. We did it like this all the time. The other two didn't.

Another white man, called Tom Rawlins, came here for a while, then he left. Jack Long came here then, bringing men to work. Oh, those horses just had those men for dinner! They weren't used to men, you know. The horses only knew girls. Talk about bucking the men! And you know that eucalypt tree I showed you? Tinti-tinti? A horse came out from there, bucking one of the men, throwing him, head over arse, poor thing! Janet Napanangka's grandfather.

GN: Was that my grandfather you're talking about?

KN: Yes, that's the one that the horse threw [making him unconscious]. We woke him up, and bandaged him. Mrs Davis had to

Bandage-em. Mrs Davis bin take-em — what's-a-name? Wheelbarrow — that's all. Go gettem. Bandage-em, washem, make-em right. Pokem that medicine — good medicine, bush [laughter]. Me — and ah, that 'nother one, long what's that Nyinjirri? Dry one?

Yeah, Nyinjirri, mintwofella bin there again. 'Nother two fresh horses, you know — that 'nother mob again, allabout bin use-em here. Well mintwofella bin comin' up. I bin come back, 'What's-a-matter? Eh, one sick, or?' 'Beatem, horse bin beatem up.' 'Oh.' 'Oh, this wild bugger — buck jumper horses,' that Mrs Davis bin talk. 'Well, youfella gotta shootem anytime, you know. Makem good — wild bugger.' Well, mefella bin goin' up Ngarnalkurru way — everyway. I bin havem colt again. That 'nother one bin same again. Mefella bin ridem, you know, fresh horse. Well that 'nother horse bin bolt — droppem again. And him bin bolt, that man. I bin just puttem what's-a-name? Whip, you know, double one.

Well I bin makem good now, that horses. All right, holiday — Sunday. Mefella bin all day dressed up now. Walk around this creek here — everyway. Come back time. And sometime me bin think kangaroo. I bin all day chasem and killem. Mmmm. Bringem back and cookem. ❐

get the wheelbarrow to pick him up. I washed him, bandaged him up and rubbed him with bush medicine — good medicine that. I did that, with another person. We'd just come back from that dry place, Nyinjirri? bringing fresh horses with us. Well, the two of us came up, and I said, 'What's the matter? Is he sick? Did the horse beat him up?' Well, Mrs Davis said, 'Well, these horses are wild, buck jumpers, you should shoot some of them and quieten them down.' Well, we'd been riding those horses around everywhere, up to Ngarnalkurru way, everywhere. I had a colt; the other lady had one too, wild ones. Well it was one of those horses that tossed that man. So I used a whip on him, a double whip.

Well, I made those horses quiet then. All right, because Sunday was a holiday, we got all dressed up, and followed the creek, walking everywhere. Sometimes I'd think about kangaroos. I'd chase them and kill them and bring them back to cook. ❐

Snake in the hole *by Maisie Napaljarri Kitson. Linocut print, 1994*

Part Three
Changes

Army time

A small number of men from the Lander area were employed by the army during the Second World War and, for the first time since contact with whites, they had decent working conditions. They remember the time with fondness, and talk about the good food, medical treatment, and accommodation that was provided. Of particular importance was the fact that they received regular wages and lived side by side with whites. The men worked mainly as unskilled labourers and helped to construct the Stuart Highway. They were stationed at New Barrow Camp, north of Barrow Creek,[1] where they came into contact with Aborigines from other linguistic groups and regions. While there they were able to renew ties with relatives, forge new alliances and discuss ceremonial business. In the following story Molly Nungarrayi talks about the army time as a 'free time', when they could hunt bush food in the Barrow Creek area without fear, and when they tasted beer for the first time. She recounts how people from Willowra visited relations at New Barrow for initiation ceremonies. On returning to Willowra, Molly and her sister Rosie found the body of a Jakamarra who had died from a bullet wound. They fled to Mount Peake, where they learnt of their father's death at New Barrow. While the details are not clear, it seems that a court case ensued over the death of the Jakamarra, for which Molly and Rosie travelled to Alice Springs to give evidence. As was the custom in those days, Aboriginal witnesses were left to their own devices to return home.

Molly Nungarrayi

Jungarrayi and Jampijinpa joined the army. Lots of Aboriginal people were joining the army. Free time. That's olden time. After that we went to another place for a holiday. We used to travel around in Wickham's time. We went east and stayed there, near the highway, for the initiation of the sons of three Japaljarris and of many Nakamarras. At New Barrow. We went to New Barrow, near Taylor Crossing, for dancing. Japaljarri and Jakamarra got everything ready for the initiation. People gathered together from everywhere. They came to New Barrow and Taylor Crossing. This was when Wickham was still at Willowra causing trouble.

The people hunted for bush food at New Barrow, and they tasted beer for the first time. They gathered together for the dancing, and the mothers of the young men danced, danced and danced, until the ceremony finished in the morning. Then they'd rest in the heat of the day. It was army time, and Wickham still lived at Willowra.

We came back to Willowra from New Barrow and travelled through Jarrajarra, walking all the way. We crossed the creek and at Ngarnalkurru we ran into a dead person, Jakamarra. He'd been shot. We ran into this trouble. We were frightened so we went to Mount Peake. We didn't know what had happened. It was while I was there that my father passed away at New Barrow.

Then the policeman came from Alice Springs to get Bob Davis, Wickham and Walter, to take them to court. They were in trouble. We think they went to jail. Rosie and I were also taken to court. It was army time. We all stayed there in jail, and then Rosie and I walked

---

[1]   See Read and Read, 1991, Part 2, chapter 4, for an account of how the army recruited people at Willowra.

back from Alice Springs to Ti Tree — all night. No cars, just walking all night! We reached the big creek, Yarlalinji, and there were a lot of people living there. They have passed away now. We held sorry business there for my father. Then we stayed at Yalyaji, a place on Anningie where there were lots of sheep. ❐

*Gathering **marntarla** (black gidgee). The branches are burned to produce ash which is then mixed with tobacco. Rose Napangardi (left), and young Gwendolyn Nangala/Napurrula with her aunties Mayleen Nampijinpa (centre) and Peggy Nampijinpa (right).*

The first time we saw an aeroplane

It was during army time that Molly saw her first aeroplane. Here Molly describes the panic caused by the appearance of the plane. She again refers to the army, the death of her father, and her journey to Alice Springs for court, and notes that it was shortly after returning home that the Parkinsons took over Willowra.

Molly Nungarrayi

WARLPIRI	STANDARD ENGLISH
Yuwa, mukurnalu wangkaja laningkaji, lanirnalu muku yukaja yirntirdi-kirra yirripirlayinikijaku first time before, mukurnalu yukaja lani ngurrpa ngurrparnalu muku yukaja. 'Nyarrpa-jarrirlipa jalanguju? Ey, kapungalpa mukupakarni waja. Yalumpungalpa yarri rdipija waja yalkirirla, pinkirrpa-jarraparnta waja, ya pinkirrpajarrakurlu, pinkirrpa-jarrakurlu. Pinkirrpa-jarraparntarlu kapungalpa mukupakarni jalanguju waja!'	Yes, we were all frightened. We all ran in under shelter to escape the aeroplane. That was the first time we saw one and we did not know anything about it. 'What's going to become of us today? It is going to attack us all! That terrible thing with two wings in the sky is coming towards us. The thing with two wings will get us all now!'
Well, yintirdi-kirrarnalu muku yukaja. Nyampupiya-kurrarnalu yukaja. Yuwayi kanunjulpa ngayi kuja parnkaja. Yuwayi, pinkirrpa-jarra kujajarra, pinkirrpa-jarra kujajarra. Ya nyampu-rnalu lani muku-yukaja yintirdi-kirra yirripirlayinikijaku. Ngarirnalu-nyanu, lani-jarrirnalu. Pinawa-ngurnalu lani-jarrija. Yintirdi-kirrarnalu muku-yukaja. Ya mukurnalu yukaja lanilki. 'Ya, ngangkayi-parntarlu pinkirrpa-jarra kajika yangka luwarni, kajika luwarni pinkirrpa-jarra palkakurlurlu ngangkayi-kirlirli.' Nyurru-wiyi yirripilayini nyanunguju. Yuwayi, ngankayi-parntarlu doctor yuwayi mukulku luwarnu.	Well, we all rushed in under the shelter as far down as we could get. It was coming fast. Yes, the thing with two wings. We came in under the shelter to avoid the aeroplane. We were frightened because we had not seen anything like it before. We all went in under the shelter because we thought it was a magical, powerful thing. 'That thing with two wings might strike us down. That has power in its body.' That's how we thought about the aeroplane in the old days — that it was powerful like a medicine man.
Mukurli-panyanu rarrlypa-jarrijarlipa lani-warnuju, mukurnalu yakarra-yakarra-pardija lani yintirdi-jangka, kulanpa yalumpuju nyarrpa-mani waja, iron one waja. Pijirrdi kulapanpa nyarrpa-mantarla waja ngayi iron one waja. Plane yalumpu iron different, nyiyajapangarra warrji-nyangulparnalu mayurlurlu, warrji-nyangulparnalu. Yintirdirlarnalu muku-	Later we came out, when we were over our fear. We had never seen anything like that, all made of iron. It terrified us because we had not seen it before.

yukaja. Yilpa kujangupiya muljungku karriyarla iron one, too much. Yuwayi. Mukurnalu lani-lani-jarrija.

Manu kajikarna yangka waja-waja-mani ngamirni kuja ngajunyangu (that's ngati, yangka kajikarna waja-waja-mani ngulaku-purdangka ngajuku ngamirni) waja, kajikarna waja-waja-mani kujanya. Well yirnalunyanu wajampa-jarrija yupuju-ngka kapu yupuju-ngkarnalu-nyanu wajampa-jarrija pina-wangu kamparru. Ya, olden time karnuru. Nganimpaku-purdangkaju turnujuku, nganimpa-patuku-palangu Japaljarri, Japanangka, ngajuku-palangumipajuku, nganimpa-patuku-palangu.

Yali-rnalu muku lani-jarrija pina-wangu. 'Lawa yarripirlayini-mipa,' ngarilparnalu wapaja pina-wangu. Well, yilparnalu manngi-nyangu, 'Nyarrpa-jarri wajarnalu, nyarrpa-jarrirnalu? Still kapungalpa muku-pakarni waja!' That's first time wajangalpa rdipija. Well yintirdi-kirra-jukurnalu muku-yukaja. Karnuru-lparnalu lanijarrija muku. Muku-lparnalu yukaja. First time-rnalu nyangu nyanunguju plane nganimpa yarri kulanganta.

Ya, pinalpalu wangkaja yapa-kari-patu, 'Kari kuja jalangu army soldier waja ka nyurru-jarri.' Ngurrju-manulkulpanganpa kujarluju lani-kirra-jala. Yuwa, soldier-warrilki palka-jarrija. Army-jala soldier kujarnijilpa yanurnu. Ngulapuru-rlipa nganayirlaji yalirlaji. Ngari ngari-wangujalarlipa yanu army-lki. Yalijikirlilparlipa army-kirralku yukaja ngalipaju. Japaljarri-warnujulu yukajarra yulpurrulku wirntinjakulku yali-kirraju.

Yuwayi nyurrurla-nyangukurrayi-jala ngamirni-kurra. Walili wirntijalku yalirlajuku. Nakamarralu wirntija, Napaljarri wirntijalpalu yulpurru-patu. Yalirlanya nyanungu-nyanguju, nganimpaku-purda-ngkajala. Yuwayi, New Barrow-rla, purdujurla. Army-li nyangka,

I was worried that I was going to lose my uncle (that's my mother's brother, my uncle's brother) that he might die. Well, we were very nervous out there in the bush, we'd never heard about aeroplanes before. Yes, this was in the olden time, poor things. Our brothers and sisters, and Japaljarri [father] and Japanangka [grandfather] were all living together as one family at the time.

We were all frightened because we didn't know about aeroplanes. We had travelled around not having heard about them. Well, we were thinking, 'What are we going to do? It might try to hide under a large gum tree.' Poor us, we were frightened. We were trying to hide. It was the first time that we'd seen an aeroplane. We thought it was for us.

Other people who knew better told us, 'Today the army is going to begin.' This is what it did to us. In fact, then the soldiers appeared. That was when soldiers came, during that period. And some of us, the Japaljarris, joined the army.

Then they started to dance for the initiation. Yes, all your uncles. Nakamarra and Napaljarri danced for the young initiates. Well, they danced there for him at New Barrow during army time, when the army was still there.

ngulangka yalirla-nalupina-pina-jarrijalku.

Pina-jarrijalkurna-lu New Barrow-rlaku, hmm, army-rlaju ya. Ngula-warnu-jangkaju yalikirra-jarrijalkurnalu trouble-karirlalkuju nganimpaju Alice Springs-kirralku. Ngula-warnurnalu, pinarnalu ngardaly-wantijarni kujarniyijala. Kankarlu-parntalku jurnkungkalku, yuwayi. Ngula-jangkajuku wardinyi-lkilparnalu muku-nyinaja nyampurlalku jurrkungkalku nganimpa-nyangurlalku yalijangka Alice Springs-jangkaju. Nganimpa-nyangu trouble-rla again. Trouble nganimpa-nyangurnalu nyurru-manu. Pinarnalu jurrkukurra-jarrija.

Ngula-warnuju Mr Parkinson-lkinganpa rdipija. That's free-lki now ngayi rumungkalku. Rumungkalkul-parnalu nyinaja Parkinson time. Ration-lkilparnalu manu, free-lkilparnalu nyinaja tarnngalku. Nyampu ngula karnalu nyina. Kirdana-kurlangurla, warringiyi-kirlangurla, yuwayi. Manu nyampu karna wangka. Nyampulkujuku karnalu nyina. Yuwayi, jungarni kalarnalu wapaja rarralypa-wiyi manu karnalu majulku nyina nyurnulku doctor-lku, yuwayi. Nyampu karna wangkamirra. Nyurru-lku ngajuluju. ❐

They got used to New Barrow during the army time. We ran into some trouble in Alice Springs, then after that we came back this way. They did Kankarlu ceremony in the bush. We went to Alice Springs. Our trouble was finished. After that we turned around and came back and stayed happily here in the same place, our own place.

Mr Parkinson joined us, and we lived freely in the time he was here. He got us supplies, and we lived without restriction. We lived in the places belonging to our fathers and grandfathers. This is what I have to say and I am finished. In those days we used to travel around young and healthy. Now we are not so well, in fact sick, and we have to go to the doctor. Now I have finished. ❐

Topsy Nangala

Ration time

In 1946 Wickham sold Willowra to Jack Parkinson, thus ending a twenty year period of violent oppression of Lander Warlpiri. Parkinson and his family maintained relatively good relations with the Aborigines, and Parkinson's time at Willowra, like the army time, is remembered by the women as 'free time': a time in which they could walk around their country, bring up their children and maintain their cultural practices without harassment by whites.

Prior to Parkinson's arrival, however, Lander Warlpiri were relocated by the Native Affairs Branch (NAB) to the newly established government settlement of Yuendumu,[1] located approximately one hundred kilometres south-west of Willowra. In moving people to Yuendumu, the Native Affairs Branch accomplished what Morton and others had failed to do; they emptied the country of Lander Warlpiri, who, since time immemorial, had given life to the land.

Forced to live with Warlpiri and Yanmajirri from other regions at Yuendumu, Lander Warlpiri became embroiled in fights — some of which proved fatal — and were determined to return to their own country.[2] They returned en masse to Willowra after the first storms of summer had fallen and there was water for their long walk home.[3] On arrival they found that a new white man, Parkinson, had taken over the cattle station.

From the beginning Parkinson sought a working relationship with the people. He employed a small number of the men as stockmen and station-hands, and a few women as domestic workers and shepherdesses. In return for their labour the Aboriginal workers received food and clothing. Under an agreement made in 1947 between the Pastoral Lessees Association and the Director of Native Affairs, Parkinson, as station employer, was also responsible for the maintenance of one wife and one child of each male employee.[4] For the most part, however, the Lander Warlpiri resumed a hunting and gathering lifestyle, their diet supplemented with rations provided by working relatives.

Between August 1949 and August 1951 a ration depot was established at Willowra,

'The old Nissan hut': this corrugated iron shed was used by white station managers during the 1960s and 1970s as the Aboriginal food store. The store stocked only basic items such as tinned meat, flour, treacle, sugar and plug tobacco. After Willowra became Aboriginal land the store was replaced by a modern refrigerated shop.

[1] For background to the establishment of Yuendumu, see Meggitt, 1962:16–29.
[2] Australian Archives (NT): F1; Item 53/628.
[3] ibid.
[4] ibid.

for the distribution of rations to the 'aged and infirm' or 'dependent' Aborigines.[5]

By the early 1950s the depredations of cattle and other introduced animals over a period of more than twenty years had begun to alter the ecology of the Lander region, and the amount and variety of food available was significantly reduced by comparison with the period prior to white occupation. The onset of a drought in the summer of 1951[6] *and the expansion of the cattle operation exacerbated the situation further. Partly in response to their changed material circumstances, and partly because of a desire for flour, sugar, tobacco, and goods such as axes and billy-cans, increasing numbers of Lander Warlpiri came in from the bush to the Willowra homestead area and, in the words of Parkinson, 'demanded to be fed and clothed.'* [7]

At the time, the government was responsible for the maintenance of unemployed 'able-bodied' Aborigines and, while they attempted to settle the latter on 'native settlements' such as Warrabri and Yuendumu, a number remained on the cattle stations. Although the practice was discouraged, station owners could apply to issue 'non-dependent' Aborigines with rations, for which they were reimbursed by Native Affairs. There were advantages for station owners in issuing rations; by encouraging people to gather together in one place pastoralists had a ready pool of labour and were able to maintain a degree of control over the Aborigines — so much, in fact, that the situation has been likened to peonage.[8] *Parkinson began rationing 'non-dependents' at Willowra,*

> *because no employment was available for them on Willowra or adjoining Stations and he wanted to prevent them from depriving the women and children of their rations. He also said that the natives would not return to Yuendumu because of ill feeling between themselves and the Yuendumu Wailbris ... This was confirmed by the natives. He argued that it was preferable from his point of view, to have the natives assembled at the homestead rather than have such a large number hunting over the run and disturbing his cattle.*[9]

In 1952 there were ten names on the ration list, but by 1954 the number had increased to seventy-one, 42 of whom were adults and 39, children.

Warlpiri did not appreciate that Parkinson received a maintenance subsidy from the government for the issue of rations, and this partly accounts for the fact that his behaviour was viewed as being in marked contrast to that of his predecessors. Instead of shooting the people, he looked after them. As Milly Nangala points out, he was a 'good man' who made it possible for Warlpiri to continue to live at Willowra and practise their culture as they wished. People felt free to hold ceremonies, and Willowra became something of a centre for ceremonial life in the region, with the the Aboriginal population doubling during the summer ceremonial cycles. When, for example, the NAB patrol officer visited Willowra in June 1954, he found that there were 'a number of natives from Phillip Creek Settlement ...

---

[5]   ibid.
[6]   ibid.
[7]   ibid.
[8]   See Rowley, 1972:206.
[9]   Australian Archives (NT): F1; 53/628.

attending a corroboree at the Station.' [10]

The Native Affairs Branch was critical of Parkinson for not complying with the Aboriginals (Pastoral Industry) Regulations 1949 (Northern Territory),[11] which required pastoralists to provide employees with accommodation, 'messing' arrangements, ablution and laundry facilities, and firewood. There was a complete lack of sanitation, and cattle troughs were used for washing. Coupled with the absence of medical treatment, ill health became prevalent.[12]

In the belief that pastoralists were deriving a good income out of the ration system, the NAB began to actively discourage Parkinson from rationing non-dependent Aborigines. Parkinson was advised that he should

> tell the natives that they cannot be maintained at the Station, and should either con-
> tinue hunting for their food, or else report to Phillip Creek or Yuendumu Native
> Settlements. [13]

The NAB then closed the 'aged and infirm' ration depot at the station. By 31 March 1954, those Aborigines who were not employed at Willowra had relocated to Yuendumu, Coniston Station[14] or Ti Tree. Only the workers, their dependent children, spouses and aged relatives remained.[15]

Over the years, Lander Warlpiri gradually drifted back to their home-land and worked for Parkinson. Using Aboriginal labour, he was able to expand and develop the cattle operation and build two homesteads, stockmen's quarters, an office and other buildings, which still stand today.

In the following accounts the women recall their lives during 'ration time', the period when they worked for Parkinson for rations.

The Willowra homestead. It was built with the help of Aboriginal labour during the period when the Parkinson family owned the Willowra pastoral lease.

---

10   ibid.

11   These regulations came into force on 1 July 1949.

12   Australian Archives (NT): F1; 53/628.

13   ibid.

14   ibid.

15   In the previous year the following were listed: twelve men and one woman employed at the station, four dependent wives and three children (Australian Archives [NT]: F1; 53/628). That there were comparatively few
women at Willowra was put down to the fact that Parkinson had a preference for employing single 'boys'
(Australian Archives [NT]: F1; 53/628).

Working for station rations

Molly Nungarrayi

Mr and Mrs Parkinson came to Willowra. Jack and Edgar, father and son, were here then. Parkinson looked after me and my family. Edgar brought in more people to Willowra. It was a quiet place, free, no trouble now. We lived here now, forever. They started giving rations and money to the people — not much rations, not rich, a little bit of flour. We stayed here, living here. We got rations, little by little, then we'd go out hunting to get more food. We were given a small amount of flour — not much, just a little. We poured flour into one billy-can and waited for water to boil in the other. Then we'd put the hot water in the flour, stir it and eat it. We called it *jupujupu*. We were given the children's rations every Wednesday and the rations for the parents at the weekend. We started eating flour and tasting tea, in return for work. Mr Parkinson used to get us to work. I used to milk the cows. I used to fill two buckets full of milk, that's cow's milk. I first worked for Edgar's mother, washing clothes and cleaning everything. Hard work, proper hard work. I wasn't paid money, nothing. That's hard work. Then, poor thing, Mrs Parkinson passed away. Poor thing, old one. Rosie and I worked for her for a short time.

Wickham and Walter, they went away forever and didn't come back. They went forever. They were wild. They used guns for Aboriginal people. That was in the olden times. Those whitefellas Bob Davis and Wickham, I don't know, maybe they passed away because they were trouble makers.

We used to live with Mr and Mrs Parkinson, with Edgar Parkinson and with Mrs Alice Parkinson. Mrs Parkinson looked after Nampijinpa and Napaljarri [Molly's daughter and niece] when they were little. Mrs Parkinson was Nungarrayi, and Edgar was Jangala. Edgar passed away and we all cried. We were sorry for him. Mrs Parkinson, Jack's wife, we cried for her also, because she used to look after us. ❐

Milly Nangala

There were separate yards for nanny goats next to the school. We used to give the kids at school goat milk. Old Yayiyayi [Edgar Parkinson's mother] used to pour the milk out in the laundry. We didn't wear good clothes, just clothes made out of old flour bags. After school we'd go out hunting for lizards, frogs and bush fruit. Sometimes we went on donkeys. There was no school here before and no fights. One of the Nungarrayis used to gather the nanny goats in the yard, and later I'd shepherd them.

We cooked our own food. We used to get a killer from the stockcamp. At first we had salted meat, and only much later did we get fresh killers. They used to keep the meat separate for my fathers who worked in the stockcamp, so that they could give some to their family. They'd bring the meat to our place. Parkinson used to call out, 'Hey, you mob can come and get more meat.' Japaljarri went and then called out to me, 'Come and see Edgar Parkinson.' We used to get the meat separately. There was some for Jampijinpa, some for Japaljarri and some for us. Ours was sent to us specially by the stockmen. I used to share meat with my sister, Nangala, when she worked with the nanny goats. We used to get the meat individually. The Nungarrayis gave meat to Japaljarris and Jampijinpas.[1]

---

[1] Nungarrayi's fathers are Japaljarris and her sons are Jampijinpas.

People came to Willowra from other places at that time. Japaljarris and Jampijinpas gathered people here because there was a good white man stopping here. The stockmen used to muster cattle. They'd bring them back this way and, after they mustered the cattle into the yard, they'd go back home and have a late supper. Then they'd go to camp. They'd sleep and then, the next morning, have their breakfast. I'd go really early in the morning to feed the nanny goats. I'd milk the nanny goats and pour the milk into buckets. The stockmen would be letting the bullocks out of the yard to eat grass. We'd get paid after the hard work.

Jungarrayi did some contracting work near Liirlpari. We walked there and I took the nanny goats with me. We had lunch and a rest on the way. We stayed at Liirlpari for a long time. I used to get rations at Liirlpari. I kept the nanny goats there, where they had plenty of grass to eat. Then we came back to Willowra, and someone else took over our jobs, milking the cows and the nanny goats. I gave my job to Nampijinpa. We used to have big fights. We used to get a lot of rations. On Wednesday we got kids' rations, and every weekend we got our own rations. ❐

Lucy Nampijinpa

I was a young woman when I started working for Parkinson. Before that I'd been walking around country to the south. Then I gave birth to my daughter and brought her with me to Willowra, to my mothers, Rosie and Molly. I went to work, and Anne, my daughter, went to school.

Lucy Nampijinpa cooking **wardilyka** *(bush turkey, bustard) at a summer camp on the banks of the Lander River, 1988.*

We used to go to work at eight o'clock in the morning and we'd work until three o'clock in the afternoon. We'd come back later at night time and work for Parkinson. Minnie Napanangka (my daughter-in-law) used to iron the clothes. I used to wash and polish the floors, making them clean. We grew older, working and working. We worked here in this place, not anywhere else.

We got rations, not much, just a small amount — tea, rice, flour and sugar. Every Wednesday was ration day for kids. Others ate damper on that day. Some of these people are still working and living here. They haven't gone to other places. ❐

The ration store

According to the Aboriginals (Pastoral Industry) Regulations, the prescribed rations for Aboriginal employees and their dependents consisted of beef, flour, sugar, tea, jam or syrup, potatoes or rice, onions or peas.[1] In addition to these items, Parkinson occasionally supplied milk, and

> *bones and fresh vegetables were cooked at the homestead to provide soup which was available to any natives on the Station ... clothing issues to branch dependents consisted of trousers and shirts to males and dresses to females each quarter and annual issues of towelling, one blanket and one sweater. The natives were always asking for needles and cotton for mending clothes.[2]*

Here Molly Nungarrayi describes how Parkinson distributed the rations from the ration store near the homestead.

Molly Nungarrayi

WARLPIRI	*STANDARD ENGLISH*
Nyampurla-wiyi kalarnalu nyurru-warnu-rla manu, yii, yalumpurlajuku kakarrarni Wurrkalirlajuku. Ruurrpa-jarrija kala wurrkalirlajuku. Kalarnalu ngariji yukajarra. Tuwa kala jajaly-yirrarnu kakarrarni-nginti. Yalinya ration-kiji kalarnalurla ngarriji karrija yalumpurlaju. Kala-nganpa, window-wanarnalu, yungu ration-ji. Kalalu jajaly-yirrarni kalalpa yakuju-kurlu, yakuju-kurlu, yakuju-kurlu, yakuju-kurlu, yakuju-kurlu, yakuju-kurlu karrinja-yanurnu yalumpu-kurrajuku. Kalarnalu tarda-yanurnu.	This is where the old ration store used to be, there to the east, where the bloodwood tree stands. It would be open on ration day for us. They used to leave it open on the east side. We would go and stand by the windows with our ration bags and get our rations through the window. We would then sit down and look through what we were given, and when it was evening we would set off home to our camps.
Kalarnalu wanta-karda wuraji-karda nyinaja, lirri-nyinaja yurturlu-kari, yurturlu-kari, yuturlu-kari yarnunjukulku. Kalarnalu ngarriji lirri-nyinaja. Tea bag-kurlu, flour bag-kurlu, rice bag-ji jalpi karinya. Ngula-kurlu kalarlipa nyinajarra-aa. Kala wanta yukajarra.	Sometimes when we came for rations we would have to wait and wait and wait for the store to open. We even had to wait until the sun went down. We used to sit in groups, waiting hungrily. We used to wait with separate tea bags, flour bags and rice bags. We used to sit around and wait as the sun went down.
'Ya, kari-nganta kutu-karirlalku ruurrpa-manu ration-ji.' Ngula manji kalarlipa rdirri-	We'd say to ourselves, 'It's late now, can't she open up?' Then she would open

---

[1] Australian Archives (NT): F1; 53/628.
[2] ibid.

yungu kanuru yapaju, ration-pardu kala yaku-yaku-yungu window-rlaju wirilki ration. Ngayi kala-nganpa yungu wirilki. Sugar-ju kala yirrarnu kujayijala kurdu-kurdu-parntakuju. Flour kala yirrarnu. Kala kartakupurdinjaju, kala yirrarnu yakuju-karirlanya. Sugar-ju ngulaju brown sugar. Kurdu-kurdu-parntakuju kala yirrarnu panunyayirni ngulajuku.

Kalarnalu kangurra, kangurra. Yapa-kari, yapa-kari kalalu yukajarni. Yukajarni ngayi kutu-karilki, no light-parnta nganayiwangurla, ngunti-wangurla ngayi kutu-karilki. Kalarnalu maturnu, maturnu, maturnu yiwarrarla jintangka ration-parnta, ration-parnta, kutu-karilki yalikirla karlarralku kujarninginti-kari-kirra ration-kirliji kartaku-kurlu, miyi-kirli, rice-kirli, plug tobacco-kurlu, panu-kurlu.

Wungungkuju kalarnalu manu jirrama-jirrama. Kalinjarlu-rlu kalarnalu manu. Jirrama-jirramayijala kalanganpa yungu, two each, two each. Jinta kala manu, jintangkarnaluyijala yangarlurlu jinta-kari, jinta-kari ration-ji. Ngulaju kalarnalu wita-wita ngarnu miyiji. Wednesday-jarrija kala. 'Ya, Wednesday-rlipa nyampuju pardi kurdu-kurdu-kurlangukulku. Kala Wednesday-yijala turnu-jarrija weekend-ji ration-kiji.' Ngulaju yakuju kalarnalu kirlka-manu Tuesday-nya ration-kirlanguju. Wednesday-jarrija kala. Kalarlipa pardija kurdu-kurdu-kurlangukuju. Kartakurlu nyangka panu, kartaku kuyu nyiya-kanti-kanti ngayi kala yungu rice, miyi, sugar, nyiyapiya ngayi jupu, manji kala rdanjarr-yungu bar soap kurdu-kurdukuju. Ngulajuku kalarnalu manu, kangu kalarnalu. Kalarnalu ngarnuyi-ii.

Tarnngalkujuku yalumpuju, tarnngalkujuku kalarnalu nyinaja. Nyampunya, nyampunya yapa kulpanja-yanurnu. Kari kala purda-purda yaninja-yanurnu yapakari, yapakari ngurukurra nyampu-kurra yangka-patu-juku mantirri-

it, and we would get up and line up by the window, poor us. We got plenty of rations, especially those who had children — they had sugar put to one side for them. They used to put flour out, and billy-cans and other bags. The sugar was brown sugar. They would give people with children a lot of rations.

We would carry the rations. Other people were still coming up. When it was dark we would set off home with our rations. We would walk along in procession on the track with no light, without even a torch, heading west to camp. It was night time when we left for the other side with our rations, with lots of billy-cans, flour, rice, plug tobacco.

Old Yayiyayi gave two of everything to married couples. She only gave one of each item to single people. We would eat a little and save the remainder until the next ration day, which was always on a Wednesday. Come Wednesday, we'd say, 'It's Wednesday, and it's ration day. Come on, let's go.' On the Tuesday before ration day we would wash our ration bags, ready for the next lot of rations. We'd get a lot of food. We'd get the children's rations on a different day. Then our billy-cans would be full up with tins of meat, everything — rice, flour, sugar, soap, lots of bar soap for the children. We'd take the food back to camp and cook it for the children.

We stayed here all our lives. We did not go to other places. There came a time when other people from other places came into our country. They kept coming and coming. I just stayed here with my sisters and sisters-in-law, right here on our fathers' land,

rlangu-rlangu nguru-kurra nyampu-kurra yangka-patujuku mantirrirlangurlangu. Nyampuju ngula karnalu marlangka nyina jukarlangu-jarraku yangkangkajuku. Ngula-kurrajuku Karrkampakurralu kulpanja-yanurnu. Kulpanja-yanurnu nyampukurraju Karrkampakurra mantirrirlangurlangu nyampukujuku.

Japaljarriki, Jampijinpa-kurlangu ngula karnalu nyina marlangka Japanangka-kurlangu yangkakujuku. Nyampu yapa kalalu yarrangurlu yarrangurlu turnu-jarrija. Wurnturu, wurnturu-ngurlu ngula kalalu kulpanja-yanurunu. Nyampunya kalu lirri-nyinanja-yani. Panu-jarrinja-yanurnulu. Tala wirili kumpu-nyanjarla nyampukurra-jarrija. Paraja-maninjarlalu p u r d a - p u r d a - n y a n j a - y a n u l u nyampukurraju. Nyampunya karnalu lirri-nyina yapaju panu-lku nganimpa nyampu-warnujala yikarnalu nyina. Nyampunya ka lirri-nyina.

Wali jalpijiki walkujuku nganimparlujurnalujana pirnti-pirntirlilki jamulu-nyangu nyampuju nguru yupuju-wanarlulku. Yapa-karirlilki Kataju-wanarlulkurnalujana manangkarrarlarlulku jami-nyangu-wu nganimpa-nyangu kuyu jukarlangu-pardukurlangu, Jampijinpa-kurlangu, Japaljarri-kirlangu. Japanangka-kurlangurlurnalujana jami-nyangulku nyampuju nguru. Too much jujuku kalurla yaarl-parntarri yapa. Ngulanya karnalu wurnturu wurnturulku nganimpaju yupuju-wanalku nyina, kujanya. Nganimpa-nyangupurnujulu nyampuju kujalu muku mata jarrija nyampukula warru-kirdi-kirdi country-rla. Nyanungu-nyangurlajukulu muku mata jarrija nganimpa-nyanguju kuyu ngapajurlangu-parduju Nakamarra, Japaljarri, Japanangka. Nyiya-kanti-kantirli muku mata-jarrija nganimpa-nyanguju nyampujuku jintangkajuku kula wurnturu, wurnturu, walku, nyampurlajuku yantarlijuku. Ngulaju karnalu nyina

where our fathers stayed and hunted. More and more people kept on coming after they heard we were getting rations and money. Today those people are still living here. We, the owners, have moved a small distance away to the bush, because people from other places are living on our fathers' sacred land. It is we who should be living on this land. The country of Japanangkas, Japaljarris and Jampijinpas. Our fathers died right around this country. Our relatives roamed this sacred country, they hunted on it and died on it. The Nakamarras, Japaljarris and Japanangkas. They all died here in one place, not far away. Right here in this place. We are still here.

On a hunting trip in her country Molly Nungarrayi breaks into spontaneous verse and performs the Dreaming for the land.

nyampujuku.

Ngarrarnalu nyina nganimpalku purdangirli-kirralku. Ngajulku ngarrarna mata jarrimirra nyampurlajuku. Nguru-ngurlu nyampungurlulku ngarrarnaju palu-pinyirra wurntururlu yupuju-ngkarlu. Kujanya karnalu nyina. Nyampuju ngawurrujarra mantirrijarra yangka mirnipala Napangardijarra yanu nyampu-wardingkimipajuku ngula-kurlangujuku Japanangka-kurlangu, Japaljarri-kurlangu, Jampijinpa-kurlangu nyampuju narrumparra, nyampu-wardingki-kirlangujuku. Ngayilki karnalu-nyarra ngirrily-nyina, karnalu-jana ngayi kurdu-kurduku nyampu nganimpa-nyanguku. Kuja karnalu ngurrju yangkaju nyina. ❐

We are still sitting here, alive. When it is my turn I will die here. I will sing myself from this place far away in the bush. We live here like this. My two younger sisters and sisters-in-law and two Napangardis, who belonged to Japanangka, Japaljarri and Jampijinpa, come from here. We stay here close to our children. Thus we sit here, happy. ❐

Rations, dingo scalping and welfare

In this account Nungarrayi provides another description of the ration distribution. She also talks about how she and her husband used to collect dingo scalps in return for additional rations. At the time, dingoes were regarded as a menace to livestock, and, in an effort to rid the country of the dogs, the government offered seven shillings and sixpence for every dingo scalp collected. It was common practice for Aborigines to hunt the dogs and give the scalps to the pastoralists in exchange for rations. The pastoralist then collected the government bounty.[1] Nungarrayi reflects that it was often hard for her people to get enough food to eat, yet, despite the hardship, they did not want to leave their country.

On 1 December 1968 equal wages were awarded to Aboriginal employees on cattle stations. Conditions did not greatly improve for most people at Willowra until 1973–74, however, when they began receiving the same entitlements as other Australians: child endowment, unemployment, and aged and disabled benefits. Thus the period of dependence on ration hand-outs ended. People were paid with cash, with which they purchased food from the store, and, as Nungarrayi remarks, 'We had a lot to eat from then on.' In the same period the Commonwealth Department of Education established a school at Willowra, and the population began to increase as Warlpiri and Yanmajirri from neighbouring areas came to Willowra.

Nungarrayi

WARLPIRI	STANDARD ENGLISH
Yaa, Edgar time-ji, ngarninja-yanurra, ngarninja-yanurra watu-watu rdakangku, rdakangku, rdakangku, rdakangku. Kalarnalurla ngarri-maturnu kartakukurlu, kartakukurlu, wita-witakurlu jampita-kurlu, jampita-kurlu, nyampupiyakurlu, kartaku wita-witakurlu. Kalanganpa ngulangka wulyurr-wulyurr-kujurnu. Kala-rnalu line-up-jarrija kartakukurlu, kartakukurlu. Juru-pungurra, juru-pungurra kala Yayi-yayirliji. Witakari witakari kala juru-pungu watu-watuju kuyujangkaju.	Yes, we used to drink hot meat soup in Edgar's time. Just hot soup. We used to put our fingers in the soup and lick them. We used to take our little cups and billy-cans and line up for the soup. Old Yayiyayi[2] used to give out the soup. She used to tip it in our billy-cans. Little by little, little by little she used to pour out the meat water.
'Kangkalu ngulajuku.' Yungkurnulku kalanganparla kujakulku kuny-kuny-ngarninjaku juru-pungu. Yirrarnu kala. Julyurl-julyurl-yirrarnu kuny-kuny-ngarninjaku yungkurnuju. Ngulaju kalarlipa jupu-jupu ngarninja-yanu rdakangku.	'That's enough,' she would say. Then she would put bones in the meat water for us to suck on. She would give us bones. We sucked and chewed the bones that she'd given us, and we'd eat the soup with our hands. In this way we'd eat, like this, like

---

[1]   See Layton, 1986:63.

[2]   Edgar Parkinson's mother. She was nicknamed Yayiyayi by the people because she used to say repeatedly 'eh, eh, eh?'

Kujarlu kalarnalu ngarninja-yanu, kujarlu kalarnalu ngarninja-yanu, kujarlu kalarnalu ngarninja-yanu watu-watuju. No miyi, miyiwanguwiyi. Watu-waturnalu live-jarrija. Ngarntajarirla, marnikijirla wiyirnalu nyinaja. Piemelon-rla, lampunu-rla, watermelon-rla. Jintangka yirrakurrurla-wiyijikirnalu nyinaja. Ngulangka-jukurnalu jintangkawiyi nyinaja-aa.

Ngula-jangka kalarnalu ngarri yarda pardija kuyu-kurlanguku watu-watuku wuraji-wuraji luwinypaju. Watu-watu kalanganpa juru-pungu, juru-pungu, juru-pungu manu piny-pinypalku kalangalparla yungkurnu yirrarnu. 'Ngulajukulu kangka watu-watujuku yungunkulu ngarni waja.' Ngarnu kalarnalu. Kalarnalu heap heap watu-watu witakari witakari ngulajuku.

'Kari-nganta killer-kurralku, killer-lku kalankulunganpa kaji-pakurnu, nyampujarrarla-ngurluju watiya-jarrarlu, yalum-purlu Dianna-kupalangurlu, Tarduku-palangurlu, Alfie-rli. Ngula-jarrarlu kalalu-nganpa kaji-pakarnu kuyu, killer. Ngayi kunaku-ngarnti, wirliyajarra-kungarnti, rdakaku-ngarnti. Ngayi ngulaku kunaku, jurruku nginyi-nginyi-wangukuyijala, jurrukuju walukuju pulukukuju.' Ngalyani-wangu, nginyi-nginyi-wangu kalapala nyanungu-jarrarlu Yayiyayi-jarrarlu muku-manu kuyuju, panujuku. Kalarnalu ngulajuku ngarnu, ngarnu, ngarnu, ngarnu kuyuju, kuna, rdaka-patu, pinti. Killer-jangka pinti yalinya kalarnalu purraja kuyuju. Ngarnu kalarnalu. Ngulanyayi kalarnalu wantakurra-manulku linjikarda. Kalarnalu purranja-wanu puyu-pinjaku-ngarnu pinti puluku.

'Kari-nganta ration-lki ya, ration-manjilki ngarrankulu mani yilarlku waja ration-lki!' Kula-nganta wiri-kari wiri-kari. Killer-pardukarirla kalalu yirrarnu corner-pardukarirla. Lawalku yali corner-

this, like this we ate the soup. No vegetables, no bread, no damper. We lived on hot soup. We didn't have any bush oranges or berries. We'd only get bush onions. We had piemelons, milk and watermelons. We just lived on those things for a long time.

The next day, in the afternoon, we'd go again for our food. Day after day it was like this; us being fed on the soup made from the meat old Yayiyayi cooked. Nothing else. A thin bone was something extra for us to take home to chew on. 'That's enough for you,' she would say, 'eat it now.' We ate. We ate the soup small amounts at a time, that's all.

Then there would be a day when the father of Dianna, Tardukupalangurlu, and Alfie killed a bull, a killer, for us over at the two trees.[3] Those two used to kill the meat, the killer for us. Only the head, intestines, legs and arms were given to us, nothing else. No tongue, no brains — Yayiyayi and her son, Edgar Parkinson, took all the good meat, all of it. We only ate, ate, ate, ate, the leftover parts: the intestines, forelegs, hindlegs and skin of the bullock. We would boil the skin until it was cooked and then we would put it out in the sun to dry up and to harden. We would then cut it into small pieces and soften it with the grinding stone. Then we'd eat the skin.

Later, Edgar would yell out to the people, 'It's ration time, you mob. Come and get your rations.' Not plenty of rations, only a small amount. They used to put the remainder of the meat in one corner. There

---

[3] The two ghost gums which stand in the paddock near the school.

pardukariji.

Jupu-jupu, tampapardu kalarlipa kurruly-kujurnu wiri miyiji flour-ju. Yu, walku, purraja kalarlipa tampapardu yalumpujuku jintakumarrarni. Kala tampangka nyanunguju wiringka, yalumpuju pumpu-maninjarla pardijarra. Yangka kalarlipa purraja tampa. Jupu-jupulku kalarlipa ngarnu ngula-warnuju, ngula-warnuju. 'Kari-nganta wirilki ngarra ka japa-kurlu-kariji yanirni purlawuju. Ration wirilki nganta kapunkulu manu, wirilki waja, too much. Kurdu-kurdu-parntarlu ngarrankulu mani wirilki.'

Jungajuku kala yirrarnu. Kuyu-pardu ngayi kala yirrarnu, ngayi two tampakungarnti ngulaju. Ngulajuku, panu-pardu-kariji lawalku. Kalarnalu nyinajarra yarnunjukukulku watu-waturla jintangkalku, kuyungka watu-waturla purrakurla. Kala-nganpa Yayiyayirliji purraku watu-watujuku yungu, watu-watujuku yungu jintajuku. Yungkurnulku kalangalpa yungu kuny-kuny-ngarninjaku.

Ngula-warnuju kalarnalu ration-ji wiripardulku manu. 'Ngayirliparla liirnpa yani ration marda wiriki japa.'

Week-pardu-karirlaju kalarnalu yanu. Kala wulyurr-yirrarnu. Kala kujarlu yangka manu japurlupiyarlu witangku ration-kirlangurlu. Kala muru-pungu yirrangurlu. 'Kari wirilkinya!' Kala pina wulyurr-kijirninja-yanu. Kala pina lurl-lurl-pungu. Kala witalku nangkuly-kujurnu. Witalku kala mukurnu-kujurnu. 'Ngulajukulu kangka.'

Kalarnalu jurru-pinjawangurlu maju-majurlu kangu karnururlu. Tampa-pardujarra jirramakungantirli kalarlipanyanu jajarnurra. Jupu-jupulku kalarlipa japakurlakariji purrajarra wuraji-wurajirliji. Ngulajangka kalarlipa line up-jarrija watu-watukulku kartakukurlu, kartakukurlu. Kartaku-kurra kala juru-pungu, juru-pungu, juru-pungu.

was none in the other corner.

We'd pour a lot of flour in the meat water to make damper. Yes, we had nothing left over, so we'd cook damper, that was all. We'd give the big damper to the family and there would be nothing left over. You know, we cooked damper and then ate only a bit of soup. We'd get more flour again next time. Edgar told us, 'Next time you will get more rations for the children.'

This is true. They'd give us only a bit of meat and two dampers. 'That's all you get, other people have nothing,' he'd say. Then we'd sit down hungry, only living on soup and meat water. Yayiyayi used to give only one serving of meat water, and some bones to suck on. We'd get more rations later on. We'd say to each other hopefully, 'Let's go, maybe we can get more rations this time.'

In another week's time we might go again. Old Yayiyayi used to tip the rations in a bag with a small ladle like this [demonstrates]. She'd put the flour in first. 'Is it a lot?' she'd ask. If it was heaped up they'd put some back in the drum. She'd shake the bag upside down then she'd start again and put a little bit in the bags. She'd tip a little bit in the bag and say 'That's enough, take it.'

We didn't ask for more, poor us, even though we only had flour for two days with nothing left over. In the afternoons we'd put water in the flour to make a flour-soup and keep the leftovers for the next day. Then we'd line up for soup with our billy-cans, with our billy-cans. Yayiyayi used to pour the soup in the billy-can. 'Take it, that's all, take it, that's enough soup and

The women's camp, Willowra 1988.

'Kangkalkulu, ngulajukulu kangka, that's enough watu-watu manu yungkurnu. Bone wajalu kangka.' Ngulaju kalarnalu ngarnu, ngarnu, ngarnu, ngarnu. Jarda-jarrija kalarnalu. Jupu-jupulku kalarnalu mungalayurruju ngarnurra. Watiyarlu kalarnalu jupu-jupu ngurrju-manu miyiji kartakukurra. Ngulalku kalarnalu ngarnu.

Ngula-jangka kalarnalu yupuju-ngawurrpakulku pirri-parnkajarra. Palkarnikilkija pirdaku yangka jurrku kalarnalu ngarnu yupuju-wana. Yirrakuru waja, ngarntajarri waja, marnikiji waja, watakiji waja, kalarnalu ngarnu. Wurramanji kalarnalu-nyanurla karlarrapurda pardija, ngulaju wunju-kurra yarla-kurra karlumparra nyampuku palkarniki pirdaku.

Ngaka ngula manjiwarnu kalarliparla ration-kiji ngunanjarla, jakati-ngunanjarla pardijarni kula-nganta wiriki. 'Tea bag wajarlipa kanyi.' Kalarlipanyanu wangkaja, 'Tea bag wajarlipa wita kanyi!' Jungajuku. 'Yantarnirli ration-ki!' Kala ruurrpa-manu. Yangka japurlu wita yungka purlawu-kurlangu manu kala kaninjarrawiyi mururra-pungu, lurl-lurl-pungu, lurl-lurl-pungu. Kala witalku wulyurr-kujurnu yapa-

bones. Take the bones too.' We'd eat, eat, eat, eat, and then go to sleep. In the morning we'd eat some of the flour-soup. We'd use a stick to stir it in the billy-can before eating it.

After this we'd go out hunting for bush food. We'd fill up on bush onions, bush oranges, conkerberries and bush lemons out bush. We'd go west for yams, spreading out a long way so that we could get enough to satisfy us.

After camping out we'd come back for rations, thinking that this time we might get a bit more. 'We might bring a tea bag this time,' we'd say to ourselves, 'We might bring a little tea bag,' [a small cotton bag like a flour bag]. That's right. 'Come for rations!' Yayiyayi would sing out. She'd open the window. She would open the flour bag and put the ladle in then shake it, shake it. She'd tip out a small amount of kungarntiji ration-kingarntiji. Kujaku jintakari jintakariki. Yangka-pardu-karirlayijala tiyi-parduju ration, nganimpa nyampurla ngularnalurla yakil-nyinajaja nyampurla walirla ngurungka. Walku kuyurlangukuju, yilararlangukuju, walkunyayirni. Watu-waturlu jintangku kalananpa palu-pungu yungkurnurlu. Rdakangku kalarnalunyanu kujarlu walirli yilpi-yilpi-ngarninjarlu. Wiyarrpa kalarnalu nyinaja ngulangka. Kalarnalu nyinaja, yii. Kula-rnalurla jilirr-manu. Jurnta-yanu kula-rnalurla walypali nyampurlaku.

Tarnngajuku walypali nyampu-wardingkiji kurlpu-kurlpujurnalujana mardanu, tarnngajulku. Ngula-purujuku kurdu-kurdu panu jarrinja-yanurnu.

Yuwa yungkurnu kala wheelbarrow-kurra manu, yungkurnu puluku. Lirrki-lirrki-pajurnu kalalu. Yii, yungkurnu yardipi, warnarri, wirliya. Yii, wheelbarrow-kurra manu kalalu yungkurnumipa yilarawangu. Ngula kalalu kangu yarrkujujukurraju.

Jungajuku kala palju rduyu-karrija maju-maju. Wirliya-jarra kala jankajarni, rdaka-jarra kala jankajarni kuyuju. Pintilki kala blanket-piya kalarnalu pupa yarrpurnu wirijiki. Yali-kirra kalarnalu panja-kujurnu blanket-piya pinti. Ngula kalarnalu-nyanu purraja, purraja, purraja, purraja. Ngula-jangka kalarnalu kujurnulku. Kilyirrparlaji wita-kari wita-kari kalarnalu pajurnu jarra-jangkaju. Witakari, witakari knife-rliji kalarnalu purraja jarrangkalku. Kilyirrparlalku yangka linjikardalku kalarnalu yirrarnu yuwali-kirra pinti puluku puyu-pinjaku-ngarntirli. Ngula-warnunya karnalu nyina nyampuju.

Nuwurnalurla sick of it-jarrija walypaliki kurlpu-kurlpuku kulu-parntaku, nyampurlaku. Kurlpu-kurlpu ngulalpa kiwayirla Parkinson nyinaja. Yayi-yayipatu

flour for us Aboriginal people, one by one. Tea was in another bag. Then we'd sit down here for a while, in this place, with no meat, no steak, nothing! We only ate soup and bones which made us sick. We used to scoop up the soup with our hands. Poor us, we only lived on that!

Every day it was like that. Truly. It was hard to get a proper feed. But as long as we had something to keep us going we were grateful. These stingy whitefellas had lived in our country for a long time, all the time while our children were growing up.

Whenever they shot a killer they brought the bad parts around to us in the camp on a wheelbarrow. They would have scraped the steak from the bones first, from the hip bones and the legs and feet. They'd put only bare bones for us on the wheelbarrow, there was no steak.

People were cooking in groups. You could see two feet cooking in one fire, and two hands cooking in another — like this. We used to spread the bullock skin out like a blanket then put the fire on top of it. We'd spread the skins out like a blanket. Then we'd watch it cooking, cooking, cooking, cooking and then take it out. When it was ready we'd pull the skin out from the hot coals then cut it into pieces. We cut it with a knife into little pieces then put some into the fat to cook. They used to use hot coals to dry the bullock skin, then put in in the bough shade before grinding it. Today we live differently.

We didn't get sick of the stingy and rough whitefellas that were here. Yayiyayi's son was stingy. Yayiyayi, Edgar, Murray and their family. Well we'd lived here for a

ngulalpalu Edgar Murray-patu nyinaja. Nyampurla walirla, ngulaju-rnalu ngula-kurlangurlaji tarnngajuku nyinaja kurlp-kurlpukurlangurla. Kalanganpa jintajuku watu-watu yungu. Ration-jilpa ngula-kurrajuku wiri-jarrinja-yanu. Nyampulpa wita-wita pulapirni-jarrinja-yanurnu. Palka-jarrinja-yanurnu kurdu-kurdumanji, ngulapurunpa ration wiri-jarrinja-yanurnu. Ngula-puruju talakulku palka-jarrija.

'Tala nganta kapunyarra yanirni, yawu.' Pipakurra manulku kalalu warru. Yii, warru pipakurra manulku kalalu walypalirliji. 'Talalku kanyarra yanirni. Yawu yapa-patukuju. Walypali wiri-wiri kanyarra yanirni nyanjakuwiyi.' Kala warru-wangkaja. Yii, ngulajuku yanurnulpalu walypalirliji. Yilpalu yapa company-wiyi nyangu. Yii, yirrarnu, yirrarnu. Pipakurra-manulpanganpa yapa company-wiyi-jiki maniyi-kiji. Kardiyarlulpanganpa kamparru leader yirrarnu. Ngula-kurramanjilkilpa sit down maniyilki yirrarninja-yanu. Ngayilkilpalu yirrarninja-yanu kardiya wiri-wirirliji welfare-rluju. Manulkulpa-rnalu, yii, ngulapurulpa sit down maniyi manu. Rdiily-yirrarninja-jarrinja-yanu ngayilpa. Yangkalpajana yirrarninja-yanu pipakurra murnma. Manulparnalu. Yii, ngulapurulpa ration wiri-jarrinja-yanu.

Kalarnalu ngarnu wiriji scalps-warnurlu. Scalps kalarlijarra pajurnuparnta. Kalarlijarra pardija, Jangalajarraju. Yii, kujapurda palkarniki miyiki. Nyampu kalarlijarra warru palu-pungu. Nyampu yatujumparra. Yii, wirliyarlu kalarnalujana warru palu-pungu, wirliyarlu, kula motorcar. Kalarlijarra milpaparnta pardija. Fresh meat kalarlijarra kangu yukuju-karirla warnapariki-ngarnti, malikiki-ngarnti, yalirrakula yatujumparra.

Kalarli-jarra wirliyaja wapaja. Ngarnalkurru nyinanya. Kalarli-jarra wapaja

long time with stingy whitefellas. They only gave us soup and bones. As more babies were born and grew up we got more rations.

'The dollar is coming for you mob, yes.' Welfare brought paper and they filled them in [government pension and child endow-ment forms]. Parkinson had walked around telling people, 'Money is coming here for Aboriginal people but first the whitefella bosses are coming to see you mob.' Then the whitefella came. He wrote things down, he wrote down all the people who were at the station without work. He wrote the names of the people who were unem-ployed. This was the first whitefella to start writing down names. It was during this time that sit-down money [unemployment benefits] began coming. That's the time that the welfare bosses began giving us money. Pensioners got money and the others got unemployment money. From then on we got more and more. First, however, he wrote lists of people on the paper, he wrote down all of us. Yes, during this time the rations were increasing.

The only time we used to get a lot of food [rations] was when my husband and I went out bush to poison dingoes and scalp them. We then brought the scalps back to the Parkinson family and they gave us food in return. We used to go out on foot, as we didn't have motorcars at that time. Jangala and I would take poison food for the din-goes.

First we went around Ngarnalkurru and Kunajarrayi area to dig poison roots. Then

wirliya Kunajarrayi-pinki-kirra. Kalarlijarra scalp-jiki, scalp maninja-yanurnu wanapariji pajarnu-warnuju. Yii, yali-warnunya kalarnalu miyiji wiriji ngarnu, tiyi, kartaku, miyi. Ngulajuku kalarli-jarra nyangu yinngirriji. Ngulajuku wirliyarlujuku kujapurda kujapurda. Nyampukula marliyarra-warnu nyinanya. Kalarli-jarra wapaja wirliyajuku pajarnu-parntaju, motorcar-wangurla. Ngarnka-pinki-kirra nyampurrakula kakarrumparra kalarli-jarra wapaja, karlumparra, yatujumparra. Karlarli-jarra wirliyajuku japaku japaku wapaja Jangalajarraju pajarnu-parnta. Miyiki kalarli-jarra wapaja. Kuyu, miyi kalalu jarrangu kijirninja-parnkaja wurnturuju yupuju-wanaju. Ngulajuku kalarlijarra pajarnu-manulku. 'Yii, kalanpa pintilki yangka maliki nyampupiya manu Jangalarluju!' Kalarlijarra miyiji ngulajuku nyangu yinngirriji, tiyiji wiriji, puulpa, yangkaji wiri-nyayirniji wanapi. Yali-warnunya kala maaly-ngarnu yapangkuju miyiji ngarringkiji. 'Yipi-yipi-ngarnirlipa kuja heap-ngka karnururlu maliki-jangka warnaparijangka pintikari-jangka!'

Ngula-kurrajuku wiri-jarrinja-yanurnu. Yii, Parkinson finish-irra-jarrija. Nyampu-ngurluju yawurra-pardija Parkinson. Yuwa finish. Kuurlu-purujuku Edgar Murray-ji kuwayilkijala. Wiyarrpa, kujalpalu kuurlu-kurralku yukaja kurdu-kurduju, nganimparnalu yaruwu-jarrija. 'Yatii, kujalpanganpa watu-watu yungu waja, kula-lpanganpa kuyu yijadurlu yungu. Kukulu-nganpa jurnta finish-jarrinja-yani, waja, kurlpu-kurlpu.' Ngula-jangka Edgar-kurlangulkurnalu ngarnu yijarduju. Ngarnurnalu ration, kuyurnalu ngarnu. Talalkupanganpa yungu wirijiki Edgar-ngkuju karnururlu ngalapinyanurlulkuyijala. Yuwayi, kurdu-kurdu kalalu kuurlu-kurra yukaja karnuru. Kiwayilkirnalu waja-waja-manu ngulakula ngurrjuju Edgar-ju. Yayi-yayi palijarrayijala

we'd go straight to another area, Ngarnka, where there were a lot of dingoes. It was there that we poisoned the dingoes and scalped them. Then we took the scalps back to the Parkinsons and exchanged them for a large amount of rations. We would share the rations with other people.

Welfare started putting children in school. It was during the time of school that one of the Parkinson brothers died. I think it was the oldest brother, old Murray Parkinson. Only Edgar was left, with his mother and wife. When old Parkinson died we were relieved. He was the one who only gave us meat-water, or who ordered Yayiyayi to give it to us. He never gave us proper meat. When Edgar was in charge of giving out rations it was all different. He gave us more than what we'd been given before and he also gave us proper bullock meat. He was good to us and we were happy with him. Then came the time when he died and when his mother, old Yayiyayi, died. We all felt sad because he was so good to us.

ngatinyanuju Edgar-kupalanguju. Palijarra kurlpu-kurlpu. Ngayi ngulajuyijala lawa-jarrija marrkurda wurlkumanu Yayiyayiji, finish.

Ngulaju-lparnalu nyinaja ngurrjulkujuku, ngurrjulkujuku, ngurrjulkujuku. Kalanganpa talalku, kuyulku, miyilki, ngayilki manyurnalku ngulakarra-karrakujuku kulpanja-yanulkulpa. Ngarnulpa-rnalu. Manyurnalkujala kurdu-kurdu-kurlangu maniyi, sit down maniyilkilpa-rnalu manu. Ngurrju-maninja-yanu-rnulkulpa.

Kuurlurlalku ngulalpa yukanja-yanu kurdu-kurduju wita-witawiyi. Nyampu ngula kalu panu kirdalku lirri-nyinanja-yani, wati manu mardukuja panuku-palangulku. Nyanunguju palkajukujala yalumpu nyinanyampa nyampuju Napangardi. Ngulaju manyurnapurlulkujalalparlipa yijardupurulkujalalparlipa nyinaja nyampurlaju tarnngalkujuku. Tarnngalkujuku yilparlipa nyinanja-aa. Kurdu-kurdulpalu ngula-puru yukanja-yanu, yukanja-yanu, yukanja-yanu, yukanja-yanu, wita-wita nyampuju. Yupukarra yupukarra ngula ka lirri-nyinanja-yani. Yii, panukirdalku ngula ka nyina.

Kula-nganta ka nguru-kari-wardingki lirri-nyina, kala nyampuwardingkijiki. Nyampuwardingkijikili panu-jarrija kurdu-kurduju. Nyampuwardingkijiki ngula kalu lirri-jarri kurdu-kurdu-warnu panu kirdalku. Yapa-kari yapa-karili-jana kanjakanja-yanurnulu-jana mirnikari-jangka. Mirnikari-jangkalu-jana kanja-kanja-yanirni jinta-kurrarlu nyampu-kurrarlu panu-kariji. Ngulalpalu nyampurla kuurlurla yukaja, pina-jarrijalpalu. Wiri-wirilpalu-jana kurdu-kurdu kanja-kanja-yanurnu ngaka. Yilpalu nyampurla yukaja, tarnnga-jarrija. Yuwayi, ngulajuku. ❐

Then other white people took over and everything changed. We lived here happy, happy, happy. They gave us money to buy meat, vegetables — everything was going well. We used to eat everything. We got money for children [child endowment] and we got sit-down money. Everything was coming along well.

The kids went to school from when they were little. That's these young men and women around here who have families of their own now. That Napangardi sitting there,[4] she was here. At that time we had everything, truly. Now we always live here. The kids start going, going, going, going to school here when they are little. Married couples, and married couples and their families are living all around. Yes, there are many fathers.

These people are not from other places, they are from here. The children are all born here. These people have been here from the time that they were young and now they have children. Other people from other places started to come in with their children. Their children go to school and learn here. Some people who had left Willowra long ago came back when their children were older. They went to school here then and stayed. That's all. ❐

---

[4] Nungarrayi is referring to Petronella Vaarzon-Morel here.

When we first used money

Faced with the plethora of changes that have occurred since the 1970s, Molly Nungarrayi reflects nostalgically on the past. She compares the apparent generosity of the pastoralists who handed out rations to the exploitative practices of some unscrupulous white store-managers in the cash-based economy of the present day.

Molly Nungarrayi

WARLPIRI	*STANDARD ENGLISH*

Warrkini-kirlangu ngulaju nyangurlu wuruly-mani, ngulaju wurulypa-kangu ka nganimpa-kujakuju, yapa-kujaku warrkini-kirlangu kurdu-kurdu-kurlangu manu nyanungurlulku kajana wuruly-kanyi. That's hungry bugger-rlu nyanungulku ka rich-jarrimirra nganimpa-nyangurlaju manirlaju. That's ka yarnunjukunyanu, kurlpa-kurlpa-jarri ka. Cheater ka kurlpa-kurlpa-jarri nganimpa-nyangukujakuju, nganimpa-nyangu maniyiparntaju.

Lawa-lkanganpa nyurruwarnu, nyurruwarnuju kujalpa nyinaja, ngunaja free-wiyi nganimpa-nyangu free-wiyi. Ngulaju ration-jilpa free yanu. Nyiya-kanti-kanti-kilpa yanu, blanket-lpa yanu, mitirililpa yanu, maniyi-lpa yanu. Nganimpa-nyanguju jalangu-jalangu wurulpa-mani ka nyanunguku hungry-lki. Wurulypa-kanyi ka nyanungurlu, wuruly-yani ka-aa. Ngaka ka yani. Wiri-maninjarla ka yani. Cheater-rlu, cheater-rlunganpa cunning ngurrju-mani. Nyanangurlulku kanyanu warlalja pajirni. Rich kanyanu ngurrju-mani, that's rich kanyanu ngurrju-mani nyanungurlu, ayi cunning. Ngulaju, maju-maju. Walypali ka rurrpa-jarri. Yangkurrarlu-nyanu kangu yapa-kari nganimpa-nyanguju again. Rich-jarrija yapa-kurlangurla, maru-kurlangurla nganimpa-nyangurla.

Ngulaju kanyanu maniyi wiri kuja kankarlumpara karrija. Rarralypa-lparnalu manu maniyi. Wirilparnalu-nyanu manu ration, wirilparnalu manu, nyiya-kanti-kanti-lparnalu manu. Wawardalparnalu

He hides working people's money and then takes off with it. He takes it away from us Aborigines. He takes it all; the working people's pay and baby money [child endowment]. Like a hungry bugger. He makes himself rich with our money. Like a hungry man. He comes and makes money for himself, then he cheats us and takes off with all our money.

White people who were here a long time ago gave things to us for free: blankets, materials, rations and dresses. They gave us things for free. Today, however, today they come to our communities and avariciously hide money and take it away. Cunning man. He cheats us but says that the money is here. He makes himself rich. That's not good for us, we don't like it. White men are hungry men. Some time ago a white person stole our money, Aboriginal money. He made himself rich with black people's money.

It was not like this before. We got things for free. We got a lot of rations for free, and materials and dresses. We paid some money for only a few of the things.

94

manu, mitirililparnalu-nyanu manu, dress, everything, nyiya-kanti-kanti. That free, wita-kari-wita-kari-lparnalu manu.

And jalangu that's do-mani cunning-lki. Cheater-rlu kanganpa cheat-mani. That's kalunyanu. Walypalipatu-karirlilinyanu kangu yangkakurrarlu again. And nganimpa-nyangu again wijingkilpalu plant-manu, wurulypa-yanu. Rich-manulpalunyanu, aya-aa. Rich-ilkili muku-yanu. Cunning-ili muku pardijarra. Maniyilpa yirraninja-parnkaja. Wutupururlu wutupururluju do-manu cunning-ilki. Nyampu karna wangkamirra.

Ngulawarnu-uu miyitingkari miyiting-karilpalu ngarrurnu wati-paturlu … Pardi-jarralkupala. Ngula-jangkaju yapa-karilki rdipijarni. Kujarlujukulpalu try-manu wati-paturluju … Manu yapa-karilki-lpalu rdakurl-pungurni. Ngulalkurnalu try-manu ngayi try, try yilpalu, try-manu yilpalu … Jungajuku cunning-jiki yanu yapa-kariji. Manunyanu wutupururlujuku. Walilpa-nganpa cheat-rlujuku cheat-manu. Nuwulparnalu manu jungarni maniyi walku. Nuwulparnalu manu cash. Only yilpa-nganpa cheat-rlujuku cheat-manu. Nuwulparnalu jungarni manu lawa, Aboriginal-rli, middle-aged-rli warrkirnirli, ngarrkangku, karntangku, warrkirnirli. Manu kurdu-kurdu-kurlangu. Nyanungu-rlulpa-nyanu jalpingki rich-manu cunning yilpa ngurrju-manu nganimpa-nyangurlu, maniyirli nganimpa-nyangurlu. Nyangu. Maru-kurlangurlu, yapa-kurlangurlulpa-nyanu rich ngurrju-manu. Rich-lpanyanu ngurrju-manu, pardi-jarra jinta-karilki. Maniyi wiri nyanjarla kala-nyanu plant-maninjarla wuruly-kangu. Kujarlujuku kalalunganpa cheat-rlu cunning ngurrju-manu. Pardijarra.

Today they play cunning tricks on us. They are cheaters, that's what they are. They cheat us. A few white people stole our money. They stole and hid our money and made themselves rich with it. They took off with all our money. This is what this story is about.

Then we had meeting after meeting where they spoke out against them. It was decided that, in the future, we would try out people we allowed to come to work, to see whether or not they were honest, because of those other ones who cheated us and did not give us money — our pensions, the workers' money, men's and women's and children's money. They only made themselves rich. They hid the money and sneaked off with it.

Molly Nungarrayi singing the country.

Manu yalumpulpa tarda-yanu jirrama-karilki. Wali ngulangka jinta jungalku karnarlu mani cash-lki. Still pukungurlu karnalu yampi. Yi, yirrarni karnalunyanu. Hundred dollars ngaju-nyangu yarri-yirrarnurnaju. Ngunaja, ngunaja jamulu. Only try ngayi kaji tarnngajapa nyina. Still kanganpa ngatingki-mani. 'Kari ngantalunyanu yirraka. Bank mantalunyanu. Safe-rlalunyanu yirraka!' Jungajuku purda-nyanyi karnalu. Yirrarni karnalunyanu junga. Jamululku karnalunyanyu nyanyi walypaliji. Ngurrju karnalu ngayi try-mardarni, and jungalku karnalunyanu yirrarni. Ngulajuku jamulu ngurrju karnalunyanu little bit. ❐

Then another two whitefellas came. Well, then we got real money, cash. Now we deposit money in the book. For example, I put in a hundred dollars and there it stays, peacefully. I try out the whitefellas. They let us know. 'You've still got some money in the bank,' they tell us. 'If you put your money in, well, the bank will keep it safe for you.' So we understand this and we deposit it correctly and we watch those white people in peace. Those good ones who we try out. We deposit a small amount of our money correctly with them. ❐

School time

In the following account Nangala describes the early days of school at Willowra. In addition to providing basic English literacy to primary school level, the first school teachers organised the free distribution of second-hand clothes and school uniforms, so that the children had clean clothes to wear at school. They also took children out hunting whenever they could, to lessen the stark divide between school and camp.

When Petronella Vaarzon-Morel arrived to teach at the two-teacher school with Jim Wafer in 1976, she found that what was expected of the teachers extended beyond providing education. At the time the Aboriginal population at Willowra was approximately two hundred and fifty, and there were approximately seventy children on the school roll.

For most people, school was the only place where they had access to showers, toilets and washing machines. There were a few recently constructed basic 'houses'. (These had no kitchen facilities and provided little protection from the elements.) However, most people lived in humpies — shelters constructed from branches, forked sticks, corrugated iron, and other materials discarded by the whites. These people had no running water, electricity or sanitation. They obtained water by digging out soakages in the river bed, from tanks that supplied the cattle-troughs, and from taps at the homestead or the school. Given people's now sedentary mode of existence, living conditions were poor, and the source of many health problems. Yet there were practically no medical facilities for the Aboriginal population. Rural Health nurses visited Willowra for a brief period every fortnight. For the rest of the time, the station manager's wife was in charge of the medical kit and was responsible for alerting the Royal Flying Doctor Service to any serious medical problems. As a result, the school teachers attended to the minor health problems of the children before school every morning, treating boils, scabies and other skin diseases. They also gave out Health Department biscuits to the children in order to supplement their diet.[1]

With regard to the children's level of education, only a few were literate in English. This was not surprising, given that few children under the age of ten were competent in spoken English. At the request of the community Jim Wafer helped establish a bilingual program, and, although there was no Departmental provision for post-primary schooling, he taught a group of teenagers how to read and write in Warlpiri. It was this group of people who went on to train and work as teachers and literacy workers in the bilingual program. Amongst the students were Georgina Napangardi and Janet Nakamarra, who assisted with the production of this book.

Janet Nakamarra as a schoolgirl, 1976.

---

[1]   Since this period, the introduction of housing, water, electricity, and a store that stocks fresh fruit and vegetables has considerably improved living conditions.

Milly Nangala

There were two Parkinson brothers and their son Edgar. It was in Edgar Parkinson's time that the school was erected at Willowra. It used to be a caravan. John Warrilow, a Japaljarri, taught there. I was living at a place called Mount Peake then. I worked with the nanny goats there until I came back to Willowra with Parkinson on a big truck. Jungarrayi, my husband, worked as a stockman. I used to work with Molly [Milly's sister-in-law] and get rations for milking nanny goats. There were lots of kids here then.

My family lived here, two Napangardis — my mother and Kathy Nangala's mother — and my father. Another Napangardi and Nakamarra were here. Wickham used to get angry with people who lived here, but people still stayed. When Parkinson was here, Sandy and Toby — two Japangardis [brothers] — and others used to work as stockmen. Two Japangardis, stockmen.

The stockyards were where the school is now. Parkinson told the men to move the yards further north, because a school was coming to that place. At first the school was one caravan, and later they started to build houses.

They used to truck bullocks from where the school is now. Older kids came to the school first, and, later on, little children. Who was that next teacher? Oh, Mr Caldicott. The teachers taught the young girls and the young boys in one room. There were no cars at the time, only Edgar Parkinson's big red truck, the Chevrolet. Everyone used to walk. They used to take the food out to the stockcamp at Eight Mile on the big red truck, food and clothing.

Jungarrayi [Milly's husband] and Jangala used to work at the school. They used to go camping out on holidays, and Nungarrayi and I used to stay with the kids at home. We looked after them while they were going to school. Jangala and Jungarrayi worked at the school for a long time [employed as caretakers and gardeners]. There were whitefellas teaching the kids. Mr Warrilow was teaching here then. He used to take the kids out hunt-

School picnic, Lander River, 1976.

ing, and sometimes we took them out with Jungarrayi. There were a lot of children coming in to school at that time. They were really good kids because they belonged to this country, to this place. Jungarrayi and I used to go out hunting with the kids and Mr Warrilow.

Mr Warrilow would give us clothes. Nowadays we buy things at the shop. Today it's a new law. The teacher gave us clothes, and we'd get rations from Parkinson, food and clothes. Each of us got clothes. We didn't only get food but blankets also. He used to give them to us free. The teachers gave us clothes for free. Later we used to wash the school uniforms. Young girls were *myall* then. We used to look after those kids at school so that they didn't fight.

Aboriginal people didn't know about teaching at school then. In the afternoon the children came out from the classroom and we'd take them home for supper. At lunch-time the teacher would give us food, and we'd sit outside on the grass with the children and eat our lunch. In the morning the children had showers before school. We'd wash the children's clothes.

It was about that time that they sent all the nanny goats away that hadn't already died. At that stage there were a lot of people coming to Willowra, and many children went to school. We didn't send our children to hospital then, and the doctors and sisters didn't check our children to see if they were sick. Our children were born at Willowra where they belong. It is the country of our grandfathers and grandmothers. Later we used to have a sister coming here every week. No, not that often.

Jungarrayi used to take the children to school each morning. The teacher gave things to him, and clothes for us. We'd eat lunch at school. The children who were carried around in coolamons were given medicine. In the afternoon we'd take the little ones home. We all went to bed and, in the morning, we'd rise and tell the children to have breakfast and get ready for school. ❐

Mount Barkly outstation school, 1988.

On travelling through country: from foot to motorcar

Since the days when the pastoralists attempted to control Aboriginal activity on the land by handing out rations at the homestead, people's freedom of movement has become increasingly constrained. Tied to the community area because of work, daily meetings, school, and the need to use the facilities of the store and clinic, people no longer pursue a hunter-gatherer lifestyle. Yet women's desire to hunt and camp out bush, to visit and care for sites on country, and to perform **yawulyu** *ceremonies away from the hubbub of the settlement has not diminished. Women are also keen to visit other places and, on the home front, they need transport to gather firewood and cart water. Motorcars are thus a much valued item. Women, however, are often frustrated in gaining access to vehicles. In this account, Nungarrayi contrasts the early days of hunting and gathering on foot to these times when motorcars are part of everyday life. She also mentions the women's efforts to obtain a car.*

Molly Nungarrayi

WARLPIRI	*STANDARD ENGLISH*
Kujakula mayi juul-juulpawangu wirliya kalarlipa wapal-pardija, wapal-pardija. Kalarlipa-aa wirliya-ku. Wardipi kalarlipa warru-pakarnu ngulya-kari ngulya-kari. Wirliya kalarlipa puraja laniwarnu. Kalarlipa puraja wirliyarlujuku no mutukayi. Kalarlipa purraku yirrarnu malurnparla yalijuku yamangka. Ngula kalarlipa yamangurlulku wapaja. Wantangku kalangalpa warru-jankaja-aa. Kalarlipa pina karrkanja-yanu yama-kurra ngayi wardapi-kirliki panu-kurlulku pulapi-kirliliki, jurlarda-kurlu waja, yarla-kurlu waja panu-kurlu. Kalarnalu yaninja-yanurnu yama-kurraji. Ngula kalarnalu purraja wurajikarda, purraja, purraja. Miyi, kuyu kalarnalu ngarnu. Yii, purra-kurlanguku yilpa wurajilki pardi. Nyampujulpa-nyanu muku jajarnu, wurajilki kalarnalu pardijarra. Wirliyajuku no mutukayi nyurruwiyi. Nyurruwiyi wirliya kalarnalu wapaja, wapal-pardija.	To be precise, we used to travel around on foot, constantly. We hunted goannas from burrow to burrow. We followed what we hunted on foot, without motorcars. We put water for drinking in the shade of bough shelters. Out of the shade the sun made us hot. We'd return to the shade with many goannas, bush honey and yams. Then we'd cook everything in the afternoon. We ate vegetables and meat and drank water. By the afternoon everything would be eaten and we'd leave. On foot always, no motorcar in the old days. We used to travel on foot.
Yukunju-maninja-yanu kalarnalu-nyanu warlulku. Kalarnalu-nyanu ngalyipi-parntarlu manurra, parrajarla karnkarlumparra-warnu ngalyipi-kirlirliwiyi, pilti-wangurlu, ngalyipi-kirlirli	We used to gather firewood as we went along. We tied it up on top of a coolamon with a vine. We had no belts but tied things up with *ngalyipi* and *witajiti* vines — only those. We carried firewood tied up with

100

witajiti-kirlirli, palkarni-kirlirli. Ngalyipi-kirlirli kalarnalu warluju manurnu.

Lawa mutukayi. Ration kalarnalu-nyanu wirliyarlulku kangu mutukayi-wangurlujala lawangku. Jalanguju karlipa mutukayirlalkujala ration-ji maninjawarnuju kanyi kapu karlipa. Walku-nyanyirni lawa mutukayi kalarnalu-nyanu kangu wirliyarlu. Yuwayi, yukunju-yukunju tiyi, miyi. Ngulajuku wirliyarlujuku kalarnalu-nyanyu kangu-uu. Kuyu kalarnalu-nyanu kangu. Jalangu, jalanguju walypali-kirlangulkujala karlipa wapaja. Ngula-jangka kalarnalu ngunaja. Kuyu, wardapi kalalu ngarnu wirlinyi-warnukurlangu yangka.

'Yalikilalu ngatipinkiji rdipijarnu kuyu-parntaju waja, yakajirri-parntaju, wanakiji-parnta.' Kalalu ngarnu, ngarnu, ngarnu. Kalarnalu jarda-jarrija. Kala-nyanu miily-miily-pakarnurra puntarnin-puntarninjarla kurdu-kurdurluju. Ngula-jangka kalarnalu ngunaja. Yarda pardija kalarnalu wirliyayijala wardapi-kirraju wirlinyiji, yarla-kurra, ngurlu-kurra. Kalarnalu wirliyayijala pardija. Kalarnalu warru pakarnu-yii yama-kurra, yali-kirra yama-kurra. Yama kaninjarrarlu kalarnalu purraja kuyuju. Wirliyarlujuku, lawa mutukayi.

Mutukayirlaju karlipa jalangu-jalangulkujala wapami. Wirliyarlujuku kalarnalu pakarninja-yanurnu. Warru karrkaja kalarnalu miyi mangarri-wangujala ngulaju. Mangarriji ngakajala kalarlipa jurrkuwana ngarnu. Ngula-ngurlukula mangarringirli jakati-ngirli kalarnalu yalumpuju-ngurlulkukula karr-karrkaja wirlinyi wirliyalku. Purlawu kala ngunaja purda-ngirli jupu-jupurlanguju. Miyi kala ngunaja, purlawu kala ngunaja. Kalarnalu yupuju-kurra karr-karrkaja wirlinyi-wurru yupujungawurrpaku kuyuku pakarninjaku wardapiki, warru karrkaja. Karrkanja-yanurnu pina kalarnalu yangka yurapitikirra. Ngulaju nyurruwiyijalarnalu ngulaju muku ngarrurnu.

vines.

No motorcar. We carried our food and water along on foot, with no motorcar. Today we carry our things in motorcars. Then, we had nothing at all, no motorcars. We carried everything on foot. Yes, we used to collect lots of tea, vegetables and meat on foot. Today we travel around in whitefellas' motorcars. Then we used to lie down. We used to eat the meat — goannas — that we got out hunting.

I'd say, 'Over there, the mothers are coming with meat, with *yakajirri* [bush raisins] and *wanakiji* [bush tomatoes].' We used to eat and eat and eat. Then we'd go to sleep. The children used to take food from each other and fight over it. After we'd slept we'd set out again, hunting on foot for goannas, yams and seeds. Having hit them [the goannas], we would gather them and return to the shade. We'd cook the meat in the shade. Always on foot, no motorcar.

Today we travel by motorcar. We used to go along catching animals on foot. We didn't carry vegetable food while out hunting. We would leave it behind and eat it when we came back. We would put the vegetable food down and leave it — we didn't carry it around with us. Flour, soup and vegetables were left behind. We would set out for the bush to hunt the things living there, to catch meat such as goanna. We used to go hunting for rabbits. As we went along we would point out all the things to each other.

101

Kala jalangu-jalangulku kula. Nyampu kalarnalu wapaja yangka wirliyajuku warru karrkaja wanakijiki maninjaku yakajirriki wardipiki. Warru karrkaja kalarnalu, warru ngarninja-yanurra kalarnalu-uu, warru pakarninjarla purraja yamangkarlu. Kalarnalu lunja-purraja. Ngula-jangka kalarnalu munjurlarri kanja-yanu wirliyarlujuku jurrku-kurrarluju nganimparluju. Yilkipakayini kalarnalu manu wirliyarlujuku. Wirliyarlujuku kalarnalu warru karrkaja.

Jakati-wapaja kalarnalu. Wardapilki kalarnalu-nyanu pakarninja-yanurra. Marnikijilki kalarnalu pulapi pajurnu kartaku-kurra, parraja-kurra, ngami-kirra. Ngula-warnu kalarnalu-nyanu kalarra rdanjarr-kanja-yanu, yukunju ngayi kanja-yanu wardapilki. Ngulangkaju marnikiji-rlaju kalarnalu ngarnu yama-wanaju yulpayi-wanarlangu kurlarni-ngirntirli. Nyampurlalu kapu kalarnalu ngarnu yulpayi-wanarluju yamangkarluju kuyu. Ngula-jangka kalarnalu pina-yanu jurrku-kurra yangka. Ngunaja kalarnalu.

Ngula-jangka kalarnalu yantarlilki nyinajayi-ii. 'Jukurraku-ngarntirlipa nyina kuja matangka, kuja jukurralku karlipa yani wirlinyiji wardapikiji kuyukuju.'

Ngunaja kalarnalu. Miyi, tiyi kalarnalu ngarnu. Ngula-jankga kalarnalu yarda pardija wirlinyiji yantarli-warnuju, yantarli-warnuju. 'Kari-ngantarlipa wirlinyilki yani, ngulajukurlipa pirrarniji yantarliji nyinaja. Wirlinyilkirilpa yani.' Wirlinyirliki kalarnalu warru pakarnu-yii ngulapuru marnikiji, ngulapuru wardapi, marnikiji ngulapuru. 'Ngukujangka yamangurlu nyampungurlurlipa pajirni marnikijij waja, warru pajirni.' 'Ngulapuru wardapi-kirra karnalu nganimpajau kuja karrka kuyukurra, warru pakarni karnalu.' Tarnngajuku warru pakarnu kalarnalu-yi.

Marnikiji kalarnalu yantarlirlilki

Today we do not travel like that. We do not go around on foot collecting wanakiji, yakajirri and goannas. We used to go along gathering and eating, hunting animals and cooking them in the shade. We would cook things together. We'd carry the cooked meat back to our camps on foot. We would leave things at the camp.

We'd hunt in circles, looking for goannas and catching them as we went along. We would pick *marnikiji* [conkerberries] and fill up our billy-cans, coolamons or water-carriers with them. From there we would travel to the west, carrying quantities of goannas and marnikiji. We would eat the meat in the shade by a river bed to the south. Then we'd return to the same place and sleep there.

We'd stay in the camp for a day if we were tired, then the next day we'd go hunting for goannas, for meat. We'd sleep. We'd drink tea and eat vegetables. Then we'd set off hunting again from our home camp. I'd say, 'Let's go hunting again because yesterday we stayed in camp. Let's go hunting.' At that time we used to go around hunting for marnikiji and for goannas. While picking marnikiji in the shade at that place, we'd also hunt and catch goannas in the area.

Back in camp we would winnow the

kupurnu-uu yulpangku manu kartaku-kurra. Parrajarlu kalarnalu luwarnu, yamangkarlu-yi-yi luwarnu, luwarnu, luwarnu. Ngula-puru kalalu wardapi kangurnu, kangurnu yangka yama-kurrarlu kuyu. Purraja kalalu. 'Purrayarra ngantalu ya kuyu!' Marnikiji ngayi kala yukunjulku karrija.

Wirliya-jangkajuku, lawa mutukayi, wirliya, ngayi walku. Yirrka-[Edgar]-kurlangurla, Christine-kurlangurlarnalu nyinaja-aa, lawa mutukayi. Kujajuku kuurlu start-jarrija lawa mutukayi. Mutukayirliji yalinya kalalunganpa kangu jintaku-jintaku kuurlu-wardingkikirlilki walypalirli, kardiyangku kuurlu-wardingkikirlilki. Yalikarikurralpa lirriyinja-yanurnu. Mutukayirlilki-nganpa, kangulpalunganpa. Ngula-jangka wirlinyilki kalalu-nganpa kangu mirrijiniki. Bush medicine-ki kalanganpa kangu. Ngarlkirdi-kirra, everything-kirra kalanganpa kangu. Bush medicine-ki kalarnalu-jana jarala-pina-pina-yungu walypaliji. Kala karrujuku yawulyukulku kalalunganpa kangu. Yalikirrajukurnalu mutukayi-kirra-jarrija.

Tarnngalkujuku yalumpuju, tarnngalku mutukayirla ngula karnalu wapaja. Karnalu-nyarra, kankulu-nganpa ngarningki kanyi yangka. Nyuntulkunpa-nganpa Napangardipardu yinpanganpa pina kurlurr-mardarnu, yinpanganpa nyuntulku Napangardi karnuru. Napanangkarluwi-yilpa-nganpa kangu-uu kaji nganta mani yawulyu mutukayi Napanangkarluju America-wardingkirliji.

Ngulangkulku, ngulangkulku yawulyu mutukayiyijala ngarrarnalu-nyanu manu-uu. Warlarljarluyijala yawulyurlarlu

marnikiji, cleaning out the leaves and placing the berries in a container. We would winnow them in a coolamon again and again. We would also have brought back goannas to the shade where we'd cook the meat. 'Go on, cook that meat!' Marnikiji always grow in large quantities.

Always on foot. No motorcar. Only feet. We used to stay at Edgar's place and Christine's place with no motorcar. At that time school started. Sometimes the white teachers drove us around in a motorcar. A lot of us went in that vehicle. They drove us. They would take us hunting, especially for bush medicine. They'd take us out for witchetty grubs and all sorts of things. We would teach them about bush medicine. They'd take us to the creek by car for *yawulyu* [women's ceremonies].

It continued like this for a long time. For a long time we travelled around by car. We take you, and you take us like that. You, little Napangardi,[1] you dear thing, you helped us with yawulyu. Napanangka first drove us for yawulyu in her car, Napanangka, the American.[2]

Then we got a motorcar for yawulyu — we Aboriginal people and our families — to go to yawulyu and dancing. We bought

[1] In 1988 Napangardi, Petronella Vaarzon-Morel, returned to Willowra to conduct research with the women. The Australian Institute of Aboriginal Studies supplied a vehicle for her work, which was used to take women hunting and camping out in their country, to help them collect firewood and water for their camps, to move camps to dry ground when it rained, and to ferry older women to and from the clinic and shop.
[2] Megan Dail-Jones, a dance ethnographer who conducted research with the women.

wirntinjarlarlu, yawulyurla wirntinjarlarlu manurnalu-nyanu jalpingki, kula yapangku Council-rlupuka, kula watiya-ngki watingki lawa. Mardukuja-paturlurnalu-nyanu manu jalpingki yawulyu mutukayiji wirntinjarlu. Yawulyurlarlurnalu-nyanu manu, no maniyirli, lawa yawulyumiparlu.

Wirliyajarrayi japu, Wirliyajarrayi japurnalu manu yawulyu mutukayiji. Ngula-parntajukurnalu wapaja-yi. Tarnngajuku-rnalu kangu-uu warlaljaju yawulyurlu mutukayiji kujarnalu manu-yi, kula maniyirli, yawulyurlu. Yawulyu mutukayi-rnalu manu wirntinjaku.

Wapajarnalu, wapajarnalu, wapajarnalu tarnngajuku ngulangkaju-rnalu wapaja, wapaja, wapaja-aa tarnngajuku. Ngulangkaji-yi puruku-jarrija-nganpa. Ngakalkunganpa jurnta-puruku-jarrija mutukayi warlarljajuku nganimpa-nyanguju yawulyu mutukayiji. Ngula-warnuju, 'Walkulku-yawu kari-ngantangalpa jurnta-puruku-jarrija mutukayi palkarniji nyampuju mardukuja-kurlanguju warlarljaju waja. Kulalungalpa help-manilki waja watingkiji waja, walku. Warlarljaju nyampuju-kungalpa karnuruju jurnta-maju-jarrija.' Lawalku, finish, walku. Ngulajangkaji ngayilkirnalu nyinaja, yapa-kurlangurlalku ngayi. Ngarri-kari ngarri-kari kalarnalu warru warrkarnu. Wijikari wijikarirlalku karnalu warru warrkarni yangka yapa-karirlalku. No warlarljalku, lawalku. Wijikari, wijikarirlalkuju-yii, wijikarirlalku karnalu wapa. Ngapa kanpanganpa Napangardi-pardurlu nyunturlulkula ngaka. Nyampunyanpa-nganpa rdipija, kujakujuku Napangardilkijiki, jintalkuju-kunpa-nganpa nyuntulkujuku nganimpakuju. Ngulangkujuku. Yuwayi, ngulajuku, finish. ❐

it ourselves, without any help from the Council members or any of the men. We women ourselves bought the motorcar, not by getting money,[3] but through performing yawulyu and dancing. We bought the motorcar so that we could go out dancing. We used it for a very long time until it broke down on us. It broke down on us. Our very own yawulyu motorcar! I said, 'Our only motorcar, our only one, our women's family motorcar broke down on us!' The men didn't help us. Nothing. Our very own dear car broke down. No more. Finished. Now we either stay in one place or get lifts in other cars, not our own car, no. We have to travel in other people's vehicles. And so you have come back to us, dear Napangardi. That's what I have to say. The end. ❐

Rain is unpredictable in the Tanami but when it comes it can change the landscape dramatically: rivers flood, wildflowers bloom, and roads wash out. Here Japaljarri and some visitors to Willowra dig the AIATSIS research car out of a bog following a flash flood.

[3] That is, not from money given out by the Council or as grants, but earned by performing *yawulyu* dances.

Talking hard for our land

In 1968 Edgar Parkinson, the owner of Willowra pastoral lease, suggested to the Australian government that they buy back Willowra Station for the Warlpiri people, the original owners of the land. According to Dr H. C. Coombs, who helped in negotiations over the property,

> *Parkinson wished to sell because of age and health considerations and was anxious to protect the interests of the Aboriginal community whose help and support he believed had made it possible for him to establish and develop the property.[1]*

The property was bought by the Department of Aboriginal Affairs in 1973, for the resident Aboriginal people. It was the first pastoral property to be purchased for Aborigines in Central Australia.

In 1980 Aboriginal freehold title to Willowra was granted to the traditional owners under the Aboriginal Land Rights (Northern Territory) Act 1976. In 1981 the Willowra Pastoral Company purchased Mount Barkly, the neighbouring station, so that the traditional owners of the land — the majority of whom were resident at Willowra — could have control of, and unimpeded access to, their country.[2] A land claim was placed on the country by the Warlpiri and Yanmajirri owners, and freehold title to the country was granted in 1985. During the land claim hearings for Willowra and Mount Barkly, the traditional owners were questioned by lawyers in front of the Aboriginal Land Commissioner. They were required to give evidence of their primary spiritual responsibility as well as traditional affiliation and attachment to the land. This meant giving evidence about their traditional knowledge of the country and their families' history of use of the country. In the following account Nangala describes how the traditional owners of Willowra have continued to speak up and fight for their land.

Milly Nangala

WARLPIRI	STANDARD ENGLISH
Ya, hard-jikirlipa wangkaja, hard-jikirlipa wangkaja, wangkajarlipa wiljijiki yinga nganta law-kurra olden time-kirra early days-kirra nganta, yinga yirrakarla majardikirra. Walirlipa hard-jiki wangkaja. Wiljijikirlipa wangkanja-yanu. Still-rlipa piritiji-manu ngulangkuju wiljingki. Pipakari manu pipakarirlalpa warrulpa wangkaja. Ngulaju Land Council-rlipa wangkaja ngulaju hard-jiki, wiljijikilparlipa wangkaja kajijapalparnalu nyinjaja nyurnu-nyurnukurlangu. Ngatingkilpalunganpa wiri-wiri-manu, kirdanarlu, warringiyirli,	Yes, we have spoken continuously, strongly and stubbornly, to keep the Law and the old ways. When we might have put on ceremonial clothing, well, we went along always speaking strongly. We always preached stubbornly. On paper after paper we spoke out. We spoke out at the Land Council. We talked hard to keep the old ways and the Law, the things that belonged to our ancestors, the things that belong to those who brought us up: our mothers, our fathers and our grandparents. We keep and nurture what belongs to them. That is ours,

[1] Coombs, 1978:77.
[2] Wafer and Wafer, 1983:70.

The courtroom setting during the Willowra land claim hearing, 1980. Land Commissioner Mr Justice Toohey (left) hears Warlpiri men give evidence for their country.

yapirliyirli. Ngulakurlangu karnalu warli mardani waja, that's nganimpanyangu. Walpaliwangurlawiyi, kardiyawangurlawiyi kujalparnalu nyinaja, ngula karnalunyanu hold-mani nganimparluju. Ngulajangka not yalumpu yarrkujuju jinta no yalikurlurlungurlu too. Ngulakujurnalu hard pina wangkaja. Wangkajalparnalurla, warrarda wangkaja.

Miljanpi ngulajurnalu wangkaja wiljijilki. Nyampurla, nyampurla, nyampurlalparnalu nyinaja nyurruwiyiji, nyampurla, nyampurla, nyampurla, nyampurla. Ngulakujukurnalu-nyanurla wangkaja wiljijiki, nganimpaju nguruku warlarljakujuku, nguruku warlarljakulpa-nyanurla wangkaja wiljijiki. 'Hey kajinkili jilpi-jarri, kajinkili wangkanjawangu wrong-jarri, ngulaju karnanyarra majirdikirra pina yirrarnu.'

'Yii nganimpaju karnalu nyina, new law-

from before the white people came, that is how we were. Therefore we cherish these things for ourselves.

We always spoke out hard and well. Here. It was here, here that we lived in the past. Right here. And for this reason we always spoke up stubbornly for our land and our ancestral possessions. We would say, 'Hey, if you all slip, if you all go wrong by saying nothing, then I will send you all back to the business camp for ceremonial instruction.'

Now we live under a new law, and we

Ngarnalkurru women give testimony for their country during the Willowra land claim. Petronella Vaarzon-Morel (fifth from the right) clarifies a point for linguist Professor Ken Hale (fourth from the right) who acted as translator for the hearing.

rlalku karnalu nyina. Ngurrju karnalu wangka, miyitingijirnalunyanurla wangkanja-yanu ngurrjujuku.' Ngulangkujuku-rnalu-nyanu nguru pirrjirdi-manurnalu. Ngula-jangka yawulyurnalu rdirri-yungu. Ngulangkurnalu yawulyurlu pirrjirdi-manurnalu wiljingkijiki.

Wali ngurrju, ngurrju, ngurrju yilpalu-nganpa walypalirli kardiyarlujulpalu-nganpa ngangkarranimayi-manu yingalu nganta nguru mantarla nyanungurlulku nganta, yapa-kurlangu nganta ngurrju. Wali, lawajuku, lawajuku-nganpa jilirr-manujuku kardiyaju, kardiyajulu-nganpa jilirr-manu. Minister lawajukulu wangkaja, puta wangkajanyanurla. Nganimparnalu-nyanurla wangkaja wilji wurra, mardarnurnalu-nyanu nguru, ngururnalu-nyanu mardarnu. Yalirlalparnalu wiri-jarrija. Ngula palka-jarrijalparnalu, wiri jarrijalparnalu. Kuyungkalparnalu wiri-jarrija, marnikijirla, wirtajitirla, yulpayi-warnurla, kurdujirripinkirla, purruparntarla, nyinjirrirla, lungkardarla.

speak properly at meetings. We have attended meetings and spoken very well at them. There we have continued to preach the word of our land. There we have begun ceremonies and, by means of women's *yawulyu*, we have persistently demonstrated the correct way.

Well good, good, it has been good that white people have had to listen to us to understand that they cannot have land belonging to Aboriginal people. Well, they still don't have it. The whites have tried to persuade us, with no result. The minister. In vain they have tried to talk us around, but we have always spoken out ourselves to keep our land, the land where we grew up, where we were born and grew up, where we ate its meat, its *marnikiji* berries and other food, and where we hunted frogs, lizards, goannas and blue-tongues by its creeks. It is because of this that we always spoke out.

Ngulakulparnalurla wiljijiki wangkaja nganimpaju.

Manu puluku-parntaju-nganpa ngaka kiwayikirranganpa tarntarnngarrirlangunganpa rdipija, puluku-parntaju, purlawuparntaju. Waliparnalu kawarr-karrija yali nyanungu purlawuju pina-wangurluwiyi. Ngulaju ngula-warnulparnalu-nyanu nganimparluju follow-manu. Yalijiki kurdurrkayi-jarrija. Ngula tarnngalku new law-kurralku. Ngulaju ngulakurnalu-nyanurla wilji wangkaja nganimpaju ngurunyanuku tarnngajuku Land Council-rla, nganayirla middle age-rla, Minister-rla. Ngulajurnalu wiljijilki wangkaja ngulangkaju.

Jilirr-manulkunganpa, 'Ya, yijardu kankulu-nyanurla jungarni wangka ngurrju. This jungarni kankulunyanurla ngurrju wangka. Junga kankulu-nyanu hold-mani ngurrju nyurrurlarlu.' Yingalu nganta yapakurlangu nganta mantarla kardiyarluju.

Yii ngulangkajukurnalu-uu, rich-ilkirnalu-nyanu. Ngurrju-manulu walypaliji rich-lkinyanu nyanungu-warnurlaju nguruku. Ngulalparnalu-nyanurla wilji wangkaja. Ngurrjulu-nganparla jungarnijarrija. 'Yeah mardakalu. Tarnngalkulu nyinakayi. Yuwarlilki karnalu-nyarra ngantirni. Tank karnalu-nyarra yirrarni, windmill karnalunyarra yirrarni, yuwarliki karnalu-nyarra parnta-yirrarni, pipe karnalunyarra yirrarni, shower-room karnalu-nyarra yirrarni, toilet karnalu-nyarra yirrarni. Ngurrjunkulu yalumpu wilji wangkaja nyurrurla-nyangurla ngurungka rijimanunkulu-nyanu. Yalirlalparnalu wirijarrija. Ngula born-jarrijalparnalu, wiri jarrijalparnalu. Kuyungkalparnalu wirijarrija, marnikijirla, wirtajitirla, yulpayiwarnurla, kurdujirripinkirla, purruparntarla, nyinjirrirla, lungkardarla. Ngulakulparnalurla wiljijiki wangkaja nganimpaju.' ❐

Later we encountered bullocks and flour. They persisted in coming. We were puzzled by the flour, which we had not tasted before. From that point we sought it out, and we changed in the direction of a new law. For this reason, however, we always spoke up for our land at the Land Council, at meetings of mature people, at meetings with the Minister.

Napangardis — Peggy and Petronella snapped by Sue during research for the Mt Barkly land claim, 1981.

Then someone tried to deceive us by saying, 'Yes, it is true that you can correctly speak for yourselves and you can properly keep your things for yourselves.' And they tried to keep all that belongs to Aboriginal people. We persisted in speaking up for our land.

From then on we were to grow rich on the land that the white man had grown rich on before. They had to speak honestly to us. 'Yes, you keep it forever. We will build you houses, we will put in tanks, we will put up windmills, we will put your houses up with pipes, showers and toilets. We will do this because you have so convincingly and so persistently spoken up for your land and so made yourselves rich.' ❐

From generation to generation

Despite a history of attempts at cultural domination and dispossession on the part of the dominant European society, Lander Warlpiri continue to practise their culture and are resolved to bring up future generations of children according to Warlpiri Law. For the women, this does not mean rejecting change. Rather, their hope is that, through education, their children can take over the management of all aspects of life at Willowra, so that they can achieve a greater sense of political and economic independence.

In these final accounts Nangala and Nampijinpa talk about how they maintain the strength and continuity of their culture by teaching the younger generation in the same way that the women were taught by their parents.

Milly Nangala

We used to tell the older girls to dance in the women's *yawulyu* ceremonies. Their grand-mothers used to dance for the country called Ngarnalkurru. We taught our older girls and later our younger girls. We taught them yawulyu. We taught the boys to dance for their grandfather's *purlapa* [public ceremony]. They still dance the same way today. We also taught the children about sorry business, and we showed them how to grind seeds to make flour. In the olden days we kept our chilen strong and healthy. Now we still do the same things that we did in the olden time. Today the children still dance at yawulyu, and at purlapa ceremonies which are for everyone. They still remember their culture. ❐

Lucy Nampijinpa

The Parkinson family left this place, and Aboriginal people are holding onto the land. We are looking after it ourselves. We are still working and looking after this country, and also the pastoral and community side. We are doing everything. We have grown lawns and trees. When the kids grow older they can work at the school, at the store, at the clinic, on the pastoral side and for the community. When they finish school, their mothers and fathers or grandparents tell them to work. They speak Warlpiri and the second language they speak is English. They can read, and, if important letters come, they can read them for their parents. When we get old our children will work for us in the same way that we worked for them when they were little children.

Our grandparents and parents taught us women's ceremonies and about bush food and about the land, and we hold the Law. We know everything about Aboriginal Law now; we are strong. Now we teach the young children about ceremonies and bush

Warlpiri children learn through observation and mimicry of adults. This group are playing yawalyu. Little Nungarrayi grinds white pipe clay and applies it to Napanangka in the same way that she has seen women ritually paint children in order to make them grow strong.

109

foods. When we grow old the children can take over the Law. They know yawulyu and purlapa ceremonies. We tell them what to do, we teach them so that they understand. They listen very carefully and learn what to do — how to dance — and they understand everything we tell them. From the older children down to the little ones, they know about sorry business and the Law. They learn about it little by little as they grow up, and when they are grown up they will understand everything. ❐

Lucy Nampijinpa paints Lady Nampijinpa with yawalyu design for Pawu Dreaming.

Glossary of Warlpiri and Aboriginal English terms

allabout	they, them (more than two)
bough shade	canopy constructed from branches and used for shade
bullock	castrated bull (also used by Warlpiri to mean bull, cow)
coolamon	see *parraja*
country	land, landscape, earth; an area of land associated with a particular group of related people who regard themselves as descendants of the Jukurrpa beings who created the land
cuttem	to cut, to separate
dreaming	see *Jukurrpa*
hit	kill; strike
horsetailer	someone who takes care of the horses on muster camps
humpy	traditional shelter — a dwelling typically constructed today from branches, brush, canvas, corrugated iron, or other available material
initiation	ceremony in which boys are made into young men
Jakamarra	
Jampijinpa	
Jangala	
Japaljarri	Warlpiri male subsection term; skin name
Japanangka	
Japangardi	
Jukurrpa	'Dreaming'; the basis for Warlpiri Law and custom; the period during which the Warlpiri social, moral and physical universe was created, which has an ongoing reality through the continuity of the practices that constitute Warlpiri culture
Jungarrayi	
Jupurrula	Warlpiri male subsection term; skin name
kankarlu	post-initiation ceremony; also called high-school ceremony
kantirirri	mortuary platform in a tree
karnta	woman, wife
kardiya	non-Aboriginal person, European, white man or woman, 'whitefella'
Kaytetye	eastern neighbours of Lander Warlpiri; language of the Kaytetye people
killer	cow, bull, bullock killed for meat
kirdawarri	edible grass seed
kuluparnta	angry person; fighter
Kumunjayi	name used instead of the name of a deceased person (which cannot be used for a period of time after the death); name used instead of the names of persons or things that are the same as or similar to the name of the deceased
kurdaitcha man	person charged with the responsibility of enforcing Warlpiri Law; traditional executioner; bogeyman
kuyu	meat
longa	at, to, with
lukarrara	edible seed-bearing grass and seed (*Fimbristylis oxystachya*)
mala	western hare-wallaby (marsupial species, *Lagorchestes hirsutus*)

111

marnikiji	conkerberry, bush sultana (*Carissa lanceolata*)
mayi	isn't that right; eh?
mefella	we, us
mintwofella	we two
miyi	vegetable food
myall	ignorant, unsophisticated
munyuparntiparnti	edible seed (*Dysphania rhadinostachya*)
Nakamarra	
Nampijinpa	
Nangala	
Napaljarri	Warlpiri female subsection term; skin name
Napanangka	
Napangardi	
Napurrula	
ngalyipi	snake vine (*Tinospora smilacina*), also called *wardarrka*
ngamarna	edible root, yam, sweet potato
ngalipa-nyangu	our, ours (possessive pronoun)
nganayi	what's-a-name (filler term used while trying to remember the name of a person, place, thing, etc.)
ngapiri	river red gum (*Eucalyptus camaldulensis* var. *obtusa*)
ngarlkirdi	witchetty grub (edible larva); witchetty tree (*Acacia kempeana*)
ngarntajari	edible fruit of long-leaf wild orange tree (*Capparis umbonata*)
nulla-nulla	fighting stick
Nungarrayi	Warlpiri female subsection term; skin name
nyurnu	sick, dead
pakuru	golden bandicoot (marsupial species)
palka	existent, living, alive; body
parraja	flat wooden dish used for winnowing seeds and carrying food or babies; coolamon
Pintupi	southern neighbours of western Warlpiri; language spoken by Pintupi people
pirlarla	see *wakirlpirri*
puluku	see *bullock*
purdujurru	brush-tailed bettong (also called *yarrkamardi*) marsupial species (*Bettongia penicillata*)
purlapa	corroboree; public ceremony held for men, women and children
soakage	place in dry river bed where water can be found by digging out sand
subsection	named category of relatives, who are grouped together according to the rules of Warlpiri kinship. (Warlpiri have eight subsections but sixteen subsection terms, or 'skin names' — eight for men and eight for women. The subsection system is a kind of condensed version of the kinship system. For an introduction to the Warlpiri kinship and subsection systems, see Wafer J., 1982)
sorry business	ceremonies and ritualised practices carried out by Warlpiri after the death of a relative. (In this context, when a person is sorry, it means they are in mourning for someone)
swag	bedding, blankets

tinti-tinti	a particular bloodwood tree at Willowra
tucker	food
wakati	edible seed from pigweed/munyeroo (*Portulaca oleracea*)
wakirlpirri	dogwood, edible bean of dogwood (*Acacia coriacea*)
walypali	non-Aboriginal person, European, white man or woman, 'whitefella'
wampana	spectacled hare-wallaby (marsupial species, *Lagorchestes conspicillatus*)
wanakiji	bush tomato, wild tomato (*Solanum chippendalei*)
wankili	cross-cousin (i.e. mother's brother's daughter or son, or father's sister's daughter or son)
wardingi	witchetty grub, edible larva
warnaralpa	edible seed (*Eragrostis eriopoda*)
warringiyi	father's father, father's father's brother or sister
warripinyi	edible grass seed (*Yakirra australiensis*)
Warumungu	eastern neighbours of Lander Warlpiri whose country lies in the region of Tennant Creek; language of the Warumungu people
watakiyi	native orange, bush mango (*Capparis mitchellii*)
wita	small; small amount
witajiti	vine like *ngalyipi*
yakajirri	bush raisin (*Solanum centrale*)
yali	over there, in the distance
yankirri	emu
yankurlayi	bush plum, wild plum (*Santalum lanceolatum*)
Yanmajirri	Warlpiri name for Arandic speaking people whose country lies to the south-east of the Lander Warlpiri; language of the Yanmajirri people. (The Yanmajirri people call themselves by a name that is variously spelt Anmatjirra, Anmatyerr, etc.)
yapa	person, people (as distinct from animals or plants); Aboriginal person or people, in particular, Warlpiri
yapunta	orphan; single object; something abandoned, rubbish
yarla	bush potato, sweet potato (*Ipomoea costata*)
yarrkamardi	see *purdujurru*
yawakiyi	bush plum, bush currant (*Canthium latifolium*)
yawulyu	women's Jukurrpa ceremony; women's song, dance, or body painting associated with Jukurrpa
yinjirrpi	see *wakirlpirri*
yipirntiri	berry (*Solanum cleistogamum*)
yirrakurru	small edible bulb, bush onion (*Cyperus bulbosus*)
youfella	you (more then two)
yuwayi	yes

Glosses of Warlpiri plant and animal terms are derived from the Warlpiri Lexicon Project. For the most part, glosses of Aboriginal English terms are from Koch, G. 1993.

Place names

Alekarenge	Aboriginal community north-east of Willowra and a short distance east of the Stuart Highway, formerly called Warrabri and also known at the present time as Ali-Curung (which is a misspelling of the Kaytetye name Alekarenge)
Alice	Alice Springs
Ammaroo	cattle station to the east of Willowra and the Stuart Highway
Anningie	cattle station to east of Willowra and Mount Barkly
Banka Banka	cattle station north of Tennant Creek
Barrow Creek	Township on the Stuart Highway north of Ti Tree, former location of telegraph station
Bobs Well	well on Lander River whose Warlpiri name is Yurtuntariji
Broadmeadows	former name of Willowra Station, used during the 1920s and 30s
Brookes Soak	Yurrkuru soakage, on Mount Denison Station, also known as Brookes Well
Circle Well	waterhole in Lander River, possibly Curlew Waterhole (see *Jarralyku*)
Coniston	cattle station which shares southern boundary of Mount Barkly Station
Curlew Waterhole	Jarralyku waterhole in Lander River, near northern boundary of Willowra Station
Dingo Hole	Kunajarrayi waterhole in Lander River, to the south of Jarralyku
Eight Mile	Minapungu waterhole and soakage in Lander River
Florries Well	Yarlakurlangu waterhole in Lander River
Frew River	former cattle station east of Wauchope
Gordon Downs	cattle station in Western Australia, near Northern Territory border
Granites	site of goldfields to north-west of Willowra, in Tanami Desert
Hanson River	river west of the Stuart Highway which runs northwards through Ti Tree Station and Stirling Station
Hatches Creek	former mining area east of Wauchope
Jangan-kurlangu	waterhole in Lander River, also called Boomerang Waterhole
Jarrajarra	Kaytetye/Warlpiri country north-west of Barrow Creek
Jarralyku	waterhole and soakage in Lander River
Jinpa	site to north of Willowra
Jirringipinki	site to the west of Willowra
Jump Up Yard	former cattle yard on Willowra
Jurlarda-kurlangu	site in Jarrajarra country
Jurrpunju	site to south-west of Willowra
Kajuru	site close to Willowra
Kunajarrayi	waterhole in Lander River, also called Dingo Hole
Kunarurrpa	soakage on Mount Barkly Station
Kurrukurlangu	rockhole to east of Willowra, in Jarrajarra country
Kurrurdurdu	site near Jinpa

Lander River	river which runs northward from Coniston Station to Yinapaka, the floodout at the northern end of Willowra Station
Larlpunju	Kaytetye/Warlpiri site to east of Willowra Station
Liirlpari	site on Mount Barkly Station, also called Whitestone
Majunpa	site near Willowra
Manga-Manda	see *Phillip Creek*
Marliyarrawarnu	site on Willowra Station, also called Syphon Bore
Marrupunju	site to east of Willowra
Mawukurlangu	waterhole in Lander River, also called Bottle Waterhole
Minapungu	waterhole and soakage on Lander River, site of Eight Mile Bore
Mount Barkly	Pawu, site and mountain to the south of Willowra; also the cattle station which borders Willowra to the south
Mount Peake	see *Old Mount Peake*
Mud Hut Bore	Bore at Yardingurnangu soakage
Mud Hut soakage	see *Yardingurnangu*
Munyupanji	a site in the north-east of Willowra Station (called Minyipanji in Koch, 1993)
Muranjayi	site and area to west of Willowra
New Barrow	site of army camp north of Barrow Creek
Ngapatura	site on Willowra Station
Ngantinkipinkirla	site in Liirlpari area
Ngarlkirdi-pardu	site to east of Willowra
Ngarnalkurru	site on Willowra Station
Ngarningirri	site on Mount Denison Station
Ngarnka	Mount Leichhardt
Ngarntajariwana	site on Willowra Station
Nyinjirri	site in Jarrajarra country, east of Willowra
Old Mount Peake	site of former cattle run and homestead on Ingallan Creek, to south-east of Willowra
Patirlirri	site to west of Willowra, near Tippenbah Well
Pawu	Mount Barkly, south of Willowra
Phillip Creek	former Anglican Mission north of Tennant Creek, initially founded as a ration depot
Pijaraparnta	soakage in Lander on Mount Barkly
Pirlimanu	site on Willowra Station, also called Fotheringham Hill
Pirliwanawana	site west of Willowra Station
Pirraparnta-kurlangu	site south of Mount Barkly
Pirtipirti	site on Hanson River
Rdajirdaji	soakage on the Lander River
Rdapurdu	site north of Willowra
Sandford Bore	Ngaliyawu, a site to east of Wirliyajarrayi, former camp of B. S. Sandford
Stirling	cattle station south of Barrow Creek and north of Ti Tree
Tanami	desert which borders Willowra Station and extends to Western Australia

Taripari	see *Liirlpari*
Taylor Crossing	where the Stuart Highway crosses Taylor Creek north of Barrow Creek
Tennant Creek	town north of Barrow Creek
Ti Tree	town to the south-east of Willowra
Tipinpa	site to west of Willowra, also called Tippenbah Well (see *Patirlirri*)
Tomahawk Waterhole	waterhole in Lander River, probably Jangan-kurlangu
Victoria River Downs	cattle station to north of Willowra, west of Katherine
Wajinpulungku	Warlpiri name for Atheympelengkwe, a Kaytetye site on Hanson River, also called Baxters Well
Wajirrkinyanu	site to east of Willowra Station
Waldron's Hill	see *Munyupanji*
Wapilingki	site to west of Willowra Station
Warlawurrukurlangu	soakage in Lander River not far from Wirliyajarrayi
Warlukurlangu	site to west of Willowra Station
Warrabri	see *Alekarenge*
Warranyirrtipa	site in the Hanson River area
Wauchope	site of hotel/roadhouse between Barrow Creek and Tennant Creek
Whitestone	see *Liirlpari*
Willowra	former cattle station bordering south-eastern part of Tanami Desert, now Aboriginal freehold land; community where the residents of the former cattle station live (see *Wirliyajarrayi*)
Wilypatiparnta	site on Willowra Station close to Wirliyajarrayi
Wirliyajarrayi	waterhole in the Lander River, close to site of former Willowra Station homestead and to location of Willowra community today
Wirntijangu	site to east of Willowra Station at Mount Windajong
Yakuranji	site in Hanson River area
Yalyaji	site on Anningie Station
Yardingurnangu	soakage in Lander River, also called Mud Hut
Yarlalinji	Lander River
Yilyampuru	site close to Yinapaka
Yinapaka	Lake Surprise, north of Willowra, on the Lander River
Yinirntiparnta	site on Anningie Station
Yinjirrpi-kirlangu	site on northern part of Mount Denison Station
Yuendumu	Aboriginal settlement to the south-west of Willowra
Yurnturrkunyu	site to west of Willowra
Yurrkuru	soakage on Mount Denison Station, also known as Brookes Soak or Brookes Well
Yurtuntariji	waterhole in Lander River, also called Bobs Well

References

Berndt, R., and C. Berndt 1987, *End of an Era: Aboriginal Labour in the Northern Territory*, Australian Institute of Aboriginal Studies, Canberra.

Cole, Tom 1990, *Hell West and Crooked*, Angus and Robertson, Sydney.

Coombs, H. C. 1978, *Kulinma*, ANU Press, Canberra.

Hartwig, M. C. 1960, The Coniston Killings, Honours Thesis, University of Adelaide.

Johannsen, Kurt G. 1992, *A Son of 'The Red Centre': Memoirs and Anecdotes of the Life of Road Train Pioneer and Bush Inventor of the Northern Territory of Australia*, Hyde Park Press, Richmond.

Kimber, R. G. 1986, *Man from Arltunga: Walter Smith, Australian Bushman*, Hesperian Press, Carlisle.

Koch, Grace (ed.) 1993, *Kaytetye Country: An Aboriginal History of the Barrow Creek Area*, IAD Press, Alice Springs.

Layton, R. 1986, *Uluru: An Aboriginal History of Ayers Rock*, Australian Institute of Aboriginal Studies, Canberra.

McGrath, Ann 1987, *Born in the Cattle*, Allen and Unwin, Sydney.

Meggitt, Mervyn J. 1962, *Desert People*, Angus and Robertson, Sydney.

Read, Peter, and Jay Read 1991, *Long Time, Olden Time: Aboriginal Accounts of Northern Territory History*, IAD Press, Alice Springs.

Rowley, C. D. 1972, *The Remote Aborigines*, Pelican Books, Melbourne.

Shaw, B. 1992, *When the Dust Come in Between: Aboriginal Viewpoints in the East Kimberley Prior to 1982*, Aboriginal Studies Press, Canberra.

Terry, Michael 1930, 'A Journey through the North-West of Central Australia in 1928', *Geographical Journal*, 75: 218–224.

—— 1931, *Hidden Wealth and Hiding People*, Putnam, London.

Wafer, J., and P. Wafer 1980, *The Lander Warlpiri/Anmatjirra Land Claim to Willowra Pastoral Lease*, Central Land Council, Alice Springs.

Wafer, J. 1982, *A Simple Introduction to Central Australian Kinship Systems*, Institute for Aboriginal Development, Alice Springs.

Wafer, J., and P. Wafer 1983, *The Mount Barkly Land Claim*, Central Land Council, Alice Springs.

Young, Elspeth 1981, *Tribal Communities in Rural Areas*, Development Studies Centre, Australian National University, Canberra.

Archival sources

Australian Archives (ACT): A1; Item 1937/14097
Australian Archives (NT): F28; Item GL 478
Australian Archives (NT): F28; Item GL 481
Australian Archives (NT): A431; Item 1950/2768
Australian Archives (NT): F630; Item PL 373
Australian Archives (NT): F1; Item 1953/628.

The Oral History Series available from IAD Press

Long Time, Olden Time
Aboriginal accounts of Northern Territory history
Collected and edited by Peter and Jay Read

This collection of oral histories gives a first-hand account of the impact of white settlement on Aboriginal culture in the Northern Territory. Special features of this book include a chronology of Northern Territory history and historical notes to accompany the text.

> *This was one of the first collections of Aboriginal oral history and remains one of the most important. It is a major contribution to Aboriginal – and Australian – historiography.*
> Professor Henry Reynolds

ISBN 0 949659 58 4
1991, 168pp
$19.95

Kaytetye Country
An Aboriginal History of the Barrow Creek area
Compiled and edited by Grace Koch, translations by Harold Koch

Long ago in the Dreamtime the Moon Man and the Bird Women created Kaytetye Country. For the first time the Kaytetye share their stories — from the coming of the white man, to traditional customs and lore, to stories their ancestors told them.

> *The history of Kaytetye people has always been hidden, hidden away among the people, their land and the environment. The Kaytetye people were not sure onto whom to pass the story. At last some true hidden stories have now been passed on to all people of Australia.*
> Audrey Rankine

ISBN 0 949659 70 3
1993, 160pp
$19.95